THE COLLEGE MYTH

THE COLLEGE MYTH

Why You **Shouldn't Go To College**
If You Want to Be Successful

GENE KELLY

Published by Advantage, Charleston, South Carolina.
Member of Advantage Media Group.

ADVANTAGE is a registered trademark and the Advantage colophon is a trademark of Advantage Media Group, Inc.

Printed in the United States of America.

ISBN:978-1-59932-100-4
LCCN: 2012948249

This publication is designed to provide accurate and authoritative information in regard to the subject matter covered. It is sold with the understanding that the publisher is not engaged in rendering legal, accounting, or other professional services. If legal advice or other expert assistance is required, the services of a competent professional person should be sought.

Advantage Media Group is proud to be a part of the Tree Neutral® program. Tree Neutral offsets the number of trees consumed in the production and printing of this book by taking proactive steps such as planting trees in direct proportion to the number of trees used to print books. To learn more about Tree Neutral, please visit www.treeneutral.com. To learn more about Advantage's commitment to being a responsible steward of the environment, please visit www.advantagefamily.com/green

Advantage Media Group is a leading publisher of business, motivation, and self-help authors. Do you have a manuscript or book idea that you would like to have considered for publication? Please visit www.advantagefamily.com or call 1.866.775.1696

A myth is a belief, story, or concept that is generally agreed upon but is not based in fact. This belief can shape the direction and outcome of the lives of people for better or worse. The college myth is what I call the generally accepted belief that a college education is the most, if not only, effective path to achievement, success, and wealth, and that simply isn't true.

The problem with a myth is that, although it is certainly not always entirely false, it is often inflated with false information that is accepted as fact. The truth, which I will present to you throughout this book, is this: college is not the *only* path to success, *and, in fact, for the majority of people, it is not even the right path.* Further, for many people, pursuing a college education can actually make success more difficult.

WHO AM I AND WHY AM I QUALIFIED TO TELL YOU ANYTHING ABOUT SUCCESS?

As a kid in high school, I was basically a C+ student. I went through high school shop classes, later tested the waters of college, and then transferred to a technical school where I learned several specific trade skills, which enabled me to acquire a series of jobs.

Then I went into business for myself, leveraging those same trade skills to become an entrepreneur. Since then, I've created several successful businesses and became a first-generation multimillionaire.

Today, I'm the founder and CEO of several companies, including the Accelerated Technical Training Institute, which provides individuals with the opportunity to rapidly learn multiple trade skills so they too can seek and find their own path to success, wealth, and independence. For you this process may or may not include a college education.

There seems to be this idea that only people with the highest levels of education create success. It is also often believed that only Americans with more intelligence—even geniuses—or those with luck or the right families become successful individuals. Well that's just not true. The most successful people think out-of-the-box, sometimes going against the grain of culture, taking what are widely accepted as "facts," and exposing them for what they are really are. That is my purpose and motivation for this book.

Before going any further into *The College Myth*, I must tell you this: *I am not against higher education.* Far from it. In fact, continuous learning indeed has been a mandatory component of my success. But it is *how fast* and *what* you learn that is of paramount importance, as you will discover throughout this book.

WHY COLLEGE ISN'T ALWAYS THE ROAD TO WEALTH AND SUCCESS

Here is the truth you can't ignore. Many students graduate from college *without specific job skills*, so they aren't really qualified for any particular job. Lost, they wander through the job market looking for any point of entry, and today find themselves out of work or underemployed for far too long. This is a sad fact, considering the investment of four years or more attending college, and the investment of tens or even hundreds of thousands of dollars. This certainly is not the best return on an investment.

For most people, time and money could have been better invested elsewhere. For example, you can purchase any one of over a hundred successful franchises for less than $100,000 down, and own a business that will provide an income of $60,000-$100,000 a year, or a lot more. That's significantly more than most college graduates will make with their degrees.

COMPOUNDING THE PROBLEM

Plunging America ever deeper into the college myth, No Child Left Behind, the federal standards-based educational reform program, has only made the situation worse by preaching and demanding that the path to success for all students is to go to college. This program has led many students down the wrong path and has failed to live up to what it promised.

Historically, it was assumed that the majority of high school students *should not* go on to attend college after high school (estimates have ranged from 57 to 77 percent of all students) because it was a known fact that the education they would receive would not result in their acquiring a specific skill set, that would enable them to be employed at a significant wage level.

SO THE FIRST QUESTION YOU SHOULD ASK YOURSELF IS, "WHY AM I GOING TO, OR CONSIDERING GOING TO, COLLEGE?"

In a number of professions, such as medicine and law, it is mandatory to receive a degree in order to practice in that field. However, simply receiving such a degree is no guarantee of wealth or success.

You would be surprised to learn how many doctors and lawyers are broke and saddled with huge student loans. Many individuals with PhDs work in relatively low-paying service jobs, not exactly a path to getting rich. No, the reason you want to go to college is because you want what you think it will bring you: success, independence, and wealth.

But what if that is not the case?

WHAT EXACTLY DOES IT MEAN TO BE "WEALTHY"?

Let's take a moment and define what it means to be "wealthy." For many people, this has meant having $1 million dollars or more in net worth. Net worth, put simply, is the combined value of the assets you own, such as savings, jewelry, real estate, cars, other property, business equity, and so on, minus what you owe against those assets.

Quite frankly, today, a million dollars is not all that much money when it comes to being independently wealthy into your old age. To live the lifestyle that most of us would describe as "rich" requires far more than a million dollars—and chances are you'll never get to that level with simply a well-paying job.

Some people define "rich" as the freedom to do whatever they want with their time: to travel, pursue hobbies, or spend more time with their families. I would agree that is a reasonable definition of "rich."

So, before you choose college as a path to wealth and success, you need to decide what you want and what your objective is. Is it to get into a particular job or profession because that is your passion and to achieve that goal requires a college degree? Or is it to become wealthy as you pursue your passion?

If it's becoming wealthy while pursuing your passion, I strongly suggest that you consider a path other than college. While this may seem outlandish at first, read on to become fully informed before rejecting this concept.

CHAPTER ONE

THE COLD, HARD FACTS ABOUT COLLEGE

L et's start with a sobering statistic. Approximately 48 percent of all students who enroll in college never make it to graduation. Of those who do graduate, the vast majority do not end up working in the fields that they studied.

Often, otherwise unemployable liberal arts graduates find themselves forced to attend an occupational program or enter the workforce at the very bottom in a poorly paid job in order to gain a marketable skill.

Yes, it might seem impressive. You got a degree from the college or university of XYZ, but all it really shows is that you were a competent student. That fills a line on your resume, but it does not show you can provide the results an employer wants, which will get you a high-paying job.

Further, in deciding whether or not to go to college, it's important to consider the return on your investment, not only in terms of your money, but equally importantly, in terms of the investment of your time, which is also a form of money, as you will soon see.

The final decision of what's most important will of course be different for each individual. You need to clarify what goals you are trying to achieve and your financial objectives, and choose the path that will provide you with the highest probability of success. Surprisingly, for most people, that path is not college.

Admittedly, college can provide you with certain unique opportunities. One of the greatest opportunities is the networking you can do while attending a particular institution. Some legitimate bragging rights are also attached to having attended a big-name school, which may or may not pay off through some connection down the road. But from what I have seen, such connections are few and far between, and the return on such major investments of time and money is therefore pretty thin and risky.

Even with an Ivy League degree, such networking opportunities need to be sought out and must be weighed against the costs of earning them.

The truth is that when they attend college without a very specific objective and planned outcome, many students simply end up saddled with unmanageable debts and an education that does not lead them in the direction they want to go.

The days of going to college, getting a degree, and going to work for a large corporation with a guaranteed job and security for your whole thirty-plus-year career are gone. In my parents' time—post-World War II—having a four-year degree made a significant difference in earning capability. Today, in the twenty-first century, that no longer holds true. The belief that it does may put you into a deep financial black hole from which you may never escape.

Consider this quote from Princeton University economist, Alan Blinder: "The supposed remedy [for creating jobs] is higher education. But this view may be mistaken. The critical divide in the future may instead be between those types of work that are easily deliverable through a 'wire' [Internet] and those that are not."

Mr. Blinder's work further suggests we will encounter rising wages for people doing maintenance and repair work on US-based facilities and equipment, along with our national infrastructure. Because, quite frankly, nobody will be outsourcing our skilled trade work such as plumbing, structural welding, electrical repair, maintenance, and installation to India, China, Korea, or anywhere else anytime soon. It's just not practical or cost efficient. Those jobs need to be done by workers living in the USA.

Unfortunately, the same cannot be said for jobs in manufacturing, accounting, administrative support, software programming and others, which have been successfully sourced outside the USA. Hundreds of millions of highly educated people in countries around the world are willing and able to do these jobs for mere pennies on the dollar.

> Bill Gates attended Harvard, but he dropped out in his junior year to pursue a new endeavor called Microsoft. He was a visionary who believed in the future of the desktop computer. Was it risky or was it the smartest decision he ever made? He ended up as the richest man in the world, in the #1 spot on the *Forbes* Billionaire List for thirteen straight years.

ACQUIRING KNOWLEDGE IS THE KEY TO YOUR FUTURE, BUT IT IS THE SPECIFIC TYPE OF EDUCATION YOU PURSUE THAT COUNTS

It is difficult to know what you want to do as soon as you graduate from high school or even when you need to change your career path. Almost everyone experiences this internal conflict. And, as you gather more information on different options, your goals may and often do change. That is okay, but there is a way to go through this sorting process that puts you at an advantage.

The best method is to select a learning system, in which you can try out your interests quickly, shifting gears from one interest to another and therefore sorting out your options with speed and cost savings. Time is money, and college is a very expensive learning environment in which to make a decision on your unique, individual goals and career passion.

On my learning path, I went to junior college for about a year after high school, thinking I wanted to become a veterinarian. But as I paid my tuition, lived at home, and attended school, I did more research. I made the very important decision to actually work in a veterinarian clinic, and as a result of my brief direct work experience in the field, I realized that that particular career choice was definitely not for me.

Imagine if I had waited until I'd gone all the way through medical school for seven years before I went to check out the business side of that career and then had decided I didn't like it. I would have been stuck with more than $100,000 in loans and would have had to practice in that field, quite possibly hating it for the rest of my life.

So, my advice is to explore a number of options before committing to college and potentially a lot of debt. If you are looking for a job and a good income, going to college often isn't your best bet. Regardless of how you go about your career exploration and development, be mindful that if you want to have a lot of choices in life, build your wealth, and avoid debt, you must have the opportunity to rapidly acquire job skills that provide you with many different employment opportunities early on.

Again, while almost every other type of skill is shipped out of the country, those of maintaining and building our infrastructure will be in the greatest demand.

Countless articles appear in the news about a severe deficit in this country of competent available workers with trade skills. It is quite simply an epidemic. But in every problem, there is opportunity. This situation is an epic opportunity for job seekers and entrepreneurs to recognize the problem and solve it.

THE VALUE OF KNOWING MULTIPLE TRADE SKILLS

In my company, the Accelerated Technical Training Institute, we maintain a staff of trade experts who conduct ongoing research. As a result of this effort, we have found that the people who are most in demand are those who have a demonstrable knowledge in not just one trade, but in multiple mechanical trades, with a complete understanding of how to do many different trade tasks, thus bringing an abundance of experience to the job or their business.

Because they possess a wealth of skills, these people are secure in their jobs, even if they are managers who don't do the actual work. The very fact that they know what needs to be done and how to do it gives them excellent oversight ability. They can tell whether or not the trade work was done right, and this is what makes them the most valuable managers, and/or successful business owners. And, in a pinch, they could do the work themselves rather than delegate it, which means they will always have a job. Who can replace them?

NO JOBS SKILLS AND WRONG JOB SKILLS

So why aren't there enough people with even one trade skill, let alone multiple trade skills, to fill the current demand for these jobs?

The problem is that our country has failed to teach these critical skills to American workers. Because of budgetary pressures, traditional school shop classes have all been ripped out and replaced by computers. After all, with the No Child Left Behind mandate, everyone was supposed to become a "knowledge worker," working in a cubical, right?

For a while it looked as if it were working, but because of global competition for knowledge worker jobs, future opportunity in the USA lies almost exclusively in work for the mechanically skilled individual.

However, our traditional education system does not teach individuals the trade skills they need.

WHO DO YOU THINK ON AVERAGE MAKES MORE MONEY, THE MBA GRADUATE OR THE MASTER PLUMBER?

In today's economy, someone with a master's degree in business administration (MBA) is more than likely unemployed or underemployed, even working at a big-box store or serving coffee. Whereas, master plumbers will never be out of work in good times or bad. Sure, they may have to adjust and learn more marketing skills to get more business in a down economy, but depending on the area of the country and their level of expertise, they will also be making a lot more per hour than the MBA graduate.

Historically, people have thought blue-collar professions mean low pay and working with their hands not their minds. Nothing could be further from the truth. The demand for these trade skills, which require just as much mental skill or more as white-collar jobs, shows up in their higher-paying incomes. In 2006, the *Wall Street*

Journal stated "skilled labor is becoming one of the few sure paths to a good living."

Here is an interesting fact: all the way back in 1942, Professor Joseph Schumpeter stated that expansion and investment in higher education, beyond what the labor market demanded for white-collar workers, resulted in "employment in sub-standard work or at wages below those of better-paid manual workers." He goes on to say, "It may create unemployability of a particularly disconcerting type. For the man who has gone through a college or university easily becomes psychologically (and emotionally) unemployable in manual occupations without necessarily acquiring employability in the professional work [that he studied for]."

Wow! Could this guy see the future, or what? That is exactly where we are today, with hundreds of thousands, even millions of students graduating from college each year with no trade skills and no job prospects in the field they studied. And, if they do get a job, it is often at low wages because of the competition we are experiencing from around the world.

THE TOUGH ROAD TO COLLEGE

It can be difficult and time consuming to get into the college of your choice. Many students are not fully prepared with the information they need to be accepted into the college that is right for them. As a result, many end up in a college that will not provide them with the education they need to achieve their personal and professional goals.

Due to the excessive demand, which has been primarily fueled by the college myth and government loans, colleges, and universities currently have high tuition fees, large rejection rates, and long waiting lists. Instead of rushing to join the chaos and putting your future at risk, you need to take the time to truly investigate whether college is a necessary step for you to accomplish your goals in life.

According to the National Center for Education Statistics, more than 17.3 million students enrolled in post-secondary institutions in 2005. This is an increase of more than 3 million compared to a decade ago. The projected numbers show that college enrollment is expected to reach 19 million by 2014. More students equal more competition. Sadly, most of these students graduate with significant debt and no real marketable skills.

You have to understand that colleges are businesses too and the high demand created by the college myth, combined with colleges' deceptive tactics, has given them the power to overcharge for the true value of the product they deliver, which is simply a diploma that might help get you a job.

Just like the overpriced housing market of a few years ago that damaged so many families when it failed, the college education market is an overinflated bubble built on misinformation and debt, and it is about to pop. It is my intention that this book will be the pin that helps it burst.

It is a widely held perception that college is the path to success. This notion is constantly driving us deeper into the college myth, and unfortunately, this unchallenged perception is sending many students in the wrong direction in life. Be wary. Do not go to college on the assumption of success, and do not assume that college is the only way.

WHAT IS THE BOTTOM LINE?

You need to seek information and surround yourself with people who can answer your questions about your desired field, so you can form your own opinion and path.

CHAPTER TWO

IS COLLEGE YOUR BEST INVESTMENT?

I t's no secret that college requires a significant commitment of both time and money. Depending on your educational needs, that commitment can be worth it, but it only accounts for success in a small percentage of careers. With low completion rates and excessive competition for the available jobs, the financial risk of attending an expensive college is even higher for lower-income families struggling to make ends meet. The investment becomes absolutely unnecessary if the student is comfortable working in a high-paying career that does not require a degree.

The current situation is that many families have not saved the large amount of money needed to pay for college. Four years of tuition plus living expenses comes to a considerable amount of money that most often results in a massive amount of debt. You need to be sure that you are investing in the right education for yourself, or your child. This should be an education that makes the most financial sense in the long run.

Don't misunderstand the meaning of the very true statement, "Invest in your education." Because the word invest can be misleading, it is important that you pay attention to what is the actual return on any investment. Throwing large sums of money into "investing" in a college education may not get you the financial returns you expect.

What if, instead of incurring large student loan debt, you were able to accumulate earnings by acquiring specific job skills that you could use to get a job right away?

Four years of additional earned wages could allow you to create a financial investment, without the accumulation of debt. Not only will four years of wages allow you to invest your money, you'll gain valuable work experience. Again, I'm not suggesting that you shouldn't pursue an education, but rather that you should pursue an education that allows you to earn a good wage.

Gaining an education that provides an immediate path to a job opens the doors to many opportunities. You can:

- Earn money and begin to invest

- Gain valuable work experience

- Pursue education that is practical and relevant to the job market

Four years of college tuition is money that could be better invested. When you are not working and earning, you are exposing yourself to a loss of wages, time, and potential opportunity.

Beyond tuition, there are additional costs associated with attending a college that must be factored in: housing, food, basic clothing, extracurricular activities, and other expenses. Don't be fooled. All of these expenses add up, and the debt accumulation associated with them when you are not working can be avoided without your having to give up your chance of success.

College students now graduate with an average debt of $24,000, an amount that has grown over 50 percent in the past decade. Outstanding college loans now total over $1 trillion, an amount that recently exceeded the amount of credit card debt in the USA. Student loan debt has increased 511 percent since 1999. In addition, tuition costs have risen 439 percent since 1982. High-end private schools that used to provide grants and scholarships now opt, instead, to put students on the debt treadmill.[1]

Right now students are graduating from college with record amounts of debt ranging from as little as $10,000 to more than $200,000. When you do the math, you also have to consider the lost opportunity cost—that is, the money you aren't earning or investing.

For each day that you attend college you will lose time and money because you could be working during those critical early income-earning years.

The problem of rising college costs is global, and there is now a growing realization that the value received may not add up to the price paid.

The reality is that the true cost of college is out of reach for many families across the USA. They can only afford it by taking on more and more debt. Easy credit has put thousands of families into virtual slavery over the last two decades.

Tuition costs continue to go up, and if you even hope to graduate with manageable debt, you will need to complete your degree in a maximum of four years and make sure that you acquire skills that

1 "School Debt A Long-Term Burden For Many Graduates," by Jennifer Ludden, October 21, 2011, www.npr.org.

will allow you to get a job and start making payments quickly. In most situations, that just isn't going to happen.

Beware, Debt = Slavery

In the USA, from the 1800s until the 1940s, we had share croppers and migrant farm workers who were paid for their labor, but due to long work hours, remote locations, and lack of transportation, they had no choice but to buy their goods from the company store at highly inflated prices. But they could put their purchases on account. So, day by day, month by month, they fell further behind on their bills and became virtual slaves, having to work the fields their entire life. As a song from that era said, "I owe my soul to the company store." If your attendance at college is funded by debt, you are potentially enslaving yourself to years, decades, or possibly even a lifetime of debt payments. Beware of easy money acquired through debt.

WHO EARNS MORE OVER A LIFETIME?

There are many studies that show college graduates have higher earning potential than non-college graduates, but these "studies" are often biased and don't provide a complete picture.

The ability to invest money at an earlier age can easily fill the income gap between a college graduate and a non-college graduate. Several of the wealthiest people I know started out as auto mechanics and now own tens of millions of dollars in income-producing real estate.

It wasn't a degree that made these people successful. The key ingredient was their personal drive to become successful. Anyone can choose to use whatever skills or education they have to become successful in life.

Also, these studies do not usually concentrate on employment in the trades in which the demand for skilled workers means the potential for making a great income.

Quite simply, college may not be the only, or even best, way to develop some of the most important skills you need to succeed in life—skills that cannot be underestimated as core requirements for success:

- Time management
- Personal responsibility
- Communication
- Problem solving
- The ability to sell
- Entrepreneurial vision

According to the American Council on Education, the average amount of time needed to earn a bachelor's degree is currently 5.5 years and is increasing.

THE "UNDECLARED" TRAP

Many students dodge the whole problem of making informed choices by enrolling in college with an undeclared major. But putting off a choice isn't the same as making one.

If you go to college when you do not know what career direction to pursue, you will probably end up changing majors several times and having to take additional courses as a result. Many prerequisite courses are needed to qualify for each particular program, and often they don't transfer from one major to another. This increases the time and money you spend without any guarantee of success.

Students often change majors, and it is costly. Time is money because every course, every month, and every year, college expenses mount up. Without proper direction, college can be a financial burden and ultimately a poor investment for launching a successful career.

Graduating with the wrong degree will not jump-start your career either. If your degree will not get you the job you want, what is the point? Or, if your degree qualifies you for a job that rarely becomes available, you'll end up unemployed and broke.

Every year 600,000 students leave college without graduating. If you do not graduate in four years, you are not maximizing your return on the time and money you invested.[2]

Starting and bailing out of college without graduating can be an extremely poor investment. Imagine ending up with a big loan and nothing to show for it. More than 30 percent of all college students drop out after their first year, and nearly half who attend college do not graduate.[3] You could carry that ball and chain of debt around for the rest of your life.

Now you know the truth about the getting a college education. It is tough to get in and expensive to get out with a degree. Most

2 Boesel, D. and Fredland, E. (1999). *College for all? Is there too much emphasis on getting a 4-year college degree?* Washington, DC: U.S. Department of Education, Office of Educational Research and Improvement, National Library of Education.
3 National Center for Education Statistics – http://nces.ed.gov US Department of Education.

important, that degree doesn't guarantee your success and wealth, or even a decent job.

And, as we've seen, almost half of all students do not graduate. If you do not graduate, you are more likely to struggle with a low-paying job while trying to pay off your debts. Putting yourself into this situation by choosing a college path when it isn't right for you could become a catastrophic decision.

If you do insist on going to college, why not flip the equation by acquiring the skills needed to land a better paid job while going to college and thereby paying for college as you go and avoiding excessive debt?

> Forty-three thousand people graduate from law school each year, many with as much as $250,000 of debt. Yet the total number of jobs available for lawyers has gone down by 15,000. Salaries are falling. So where is the value in the degree? What else can they do? I hope they are good at serving coffee or asking, "Do you want fries with that?"

CHAPTER THREE

THINKING OUTSIDE THE COLLEGE BOX

Now let's step back from the assumption that you have to go to college to be a success and think outside the box for a moment.

What if, instead of spending $150,000 on a college education, you decided to invest $10,000-$20,000 in rapidly learning a trade skill so you could immediately go to work creating income?

With the difference in the money you would have spent going to college you could start a business, buy a franchise, invest in real estate, or pursue other investments.

Take starting a business for example. If you can make a business a success, it is quite probable that the income it generates will greatly exceed any job you might have gotten with a college degree.

Owning a small business, although at times very difficult, has historically been the surest path to financial success.[4]

But what do you do if you are not yet ready to own a business? Or what do you do if you have decided that college is not right for

---

4 *The Millionaire Next Door* by Thomas J. Stanley and William D. Danko, published by Taylor Trade Publishing (1996).

you, or you can't afford it? What do you do to prepare yourself to secure a job and make a good living?

To begin with, develop skills you can use anywhere, anytime. To make a good income and always be assured of a good job, you must have the right skill sets.

My team and I at the Accelerated Technical Training Institute took a long hard look at the entire employment marketplace. We hired expert consultants and conducted a careful analysis. We determined that the largest need in the overall workplace, was not so much for individuals with just one trade skill, but rather, the vast number of job openings were for people who could do multiple technical tasks—that is, people who had multiple trade skills.

What we found consistently was a high demand for a combination of seven specific trade skills, that when possessed by one individual, created an almost magnetic attraction to success and secure employment in the workplace.

This is primarily because people who are knowledgeable in all seven of these trade skills benefit from the synergy that comes from the combination of these trades and gives them the ability to manufacture, install, maintain, or repair almost anything. But individuals like this are so rare they can command top wages. These seven trade skills are what you need for a variety of reasons.

KNOWING THE SEVEN TRADES PROVIDES YOU A VIEW FROM 40,000 FEET

Possessing these seven trade skills changes the way you look at things. The blinders are off and it is as if you are looking down on the whole problem from 40,000 feet, getting a complete view of how to solve it.

If you acquire these skills, you will be rare and in demand because you are in total command of any situation. With multiple trade skills you are in the cockpit, in command, taking yourself financially and technically anywhere you want to go.

Part of the reason this works so powerfully is that there is a multiplier effect. When you know things from two different trades, your knowledge is compounded, enabling you to figure out how to handle a problem in a third, unrelated area that others who are not so highly trained would miss. Experienced tradesmen will tell you their work involves handling a new "problem" every day. They are highly paid to solve difficult problems. So, if you would like to join them and become highly paid yourself, why not get the ultimate set of problem-solving skills?

When you possess the seven trade skills, each skill essentially compounds the others, making the whole much larger than the sum of the individual parts. The result is that you can handle almost any job or repair, even those not normally handled in one of these trades. That is because being qualified in these seven trades gives you the ability to solve problems in powerful ways you didn't expect. In an almost mystical way, you find yourself able to routinely get beyond the normal "mental box" that most people find themselves in, allowing you to see problems from many different angles and rapidly develop solutions.

So now, what you've been waiting for: What are the seven trade skills that anyone who wants to be successful should possess?

Here they are:

- Electrical contracting
- Plumbing

- Carpentry

- Masonry

- Welding

- Machining

- Locksmithing

When you possess knowledge of the seven trades, there is little if anything you can't build, fix, or repair.

SO HOW CAN PEOPLE RAPIDLY LEARN THE SEVEN TRADES?

You could find a community college where you can slowly learn some of them over the course of many, many years with a high cost of time and money. Or you could try to find a traditional trade school that teaches all seven trades (if you could take the four-plus years to attend and afford the high cost too). But that's not likely. Our research showed that there weren't any such schools. Not a single one taught all seven trade skills in a single program in a modern format.

Of course it is hard enough finding a single college or school that teaches even one of these valuable trades, let alone at an accelerated pace. They all bought into the idea that the need was for "soft skills," so they long ago closed down any shop-related courses. Now they don't have the money to bring them back, even though they know it is what is really needed. Instead, they have to keep "selling what they have," even if it doesn't work anymore.

TRADITIONAL SHOP CLASSES AND TRADE SCHOOLS

Another huge problem is that the old style teaching methods of "shop-class" or "apprenticeship-training" programs no longer work.

They take too much time, often use outdated equipment, and provide too little value for all the time and money invested.

After all, you can't spend an entire semester making a wooden piggy bank or bookshelf, as many of us did back in junior high school shop class and then expect to go out and get a job as a carpenter.

Regular trade schools fail in a similar way. These schools and training programs subscribe to the old idea that the total number of hours of "butts-in-seats" produces competency in students. That is no longer valid, if, in fact, it ever was.

For instance, in a typical, hour-long shop class taught in the traditional way, you might get twenty minutes of solid instruction. This will be the actual net result after roll call is taken, and a couple of corny jokes have been cracked, not to mention that all students often have to work at the level of the slowest person in the class. But this is the model schools have followed because it is all they have available.

At a typical trade school you might be taught a few core concepts on Tuesday and have another class on Thursday, and the following week it repeats. The week after that the instructor is out sick or it's a vacation day. The end result is that you are stuck trying to take all these little bits of information that have been presented, often in a disjointed fashion, and bring them together into something you can actually use to perform the work. Good luck! A difficult task, to say the least.

WHAT ABOUT APPRENTICESHIP PROGRAMS?

Apprentice programs could be excellent if they focused on teaching efficiently and quickly. But that isn't their game. The real deal is that they gain cheap labor from the apprentice for four years.

The training in an apprenticeship is spotty at best. After all, the person teaching you is often doing so because he or she has seniority, not because he or she is a professional instructor. Additionally, your instructor may not have been taught the correct way to do the job or, more important, may not have teaching skills. And what is his or her motivation to teach you anyway? You could ultimately compete with him for his job.

And even if those aren't the issues, the idea that a trade skill takes four years to learn is simply outdated and yet another form of the college myth, holding us back, mired in the traditional way we learn skills because that is what we've always had. These ideas about how trade skills should be taught are still hanging on from the industrial revolution of 150 years ago.

No, today we can benefit from modern, proven methods of instruction.

Now let's say even if you could learn a trade skill through an apprenticeship, you would still have acquired only one trade skill. Again, the problem with knowing just one trade skill is that you are in a box. When there isn't a demand for that particular skill, or there aren't many jobs available in that particular trade, you are out of luck. Someone else is in control, not you.

If you want to give yourself the greatest number of options and experience the greatest success in life, you need to have multiple trade skills. No matter what you choose to do in life, even if you are the CEO of a major company, having these skills and the confidence they provide will put you in control of any economic or work situation, period. You really need to question what you have been told about the speed at which you can learn multiple trade skills.

Think about it for a minute. Using the apprenticeship method at four years per trade, it would take you twenty-eight years to learn the seven trades. Geez! That's ridiculous. That certainly doesn't work.

SO WHY DID I TELL YOU ALL OF THIS?

Because I am on a mission, one that I hope will change people's lives forever—the lives of people like you and the ones you love.

The mission is to fundamentally change the way and speed at which multiple trade skills are taught to individuals, so they, like me, can be confident in any situation, able to repair almost anything, possessing the ability to make a good living no matter what happens, and all the while helping to turn the economy around and rebuild America.

WHAT WOULD IT FEEL LIKE IF YOU COULD DO THAT TOO?

What would it feel like for you, personally, if you absolutely knew that you would always have a job, always be in demand, and could fix anything?

What would it mean to you to be totally self-reliant, and have total confidence in your skills?

If you want that kind of confidence and control, I would suggest you become competent in the seven trades. And, the only way to do that, without taking almost thirty years to learn through traditional education methods, is to learn those trades at an accelerated pace using modern training methods.

An exclusive system of instruction has been developed that will teach you the seven trades in just months, not years.

TAKE THIS FREE SURVEY

To find out if getting certified in the seven trade skills is right for you, take a free, personalized job profile survey by going to:

www.instanttradeskills.com

This survey was developed by a national testing institute that has provided millions of high school and college students with insight into which jobs they are best suited for.

You have to be smart about how you spend time and money on getting the right skills.

All along, I've said to be careful about what you spend your money and time on, and question the myth in this country that to be successful you have to go to college. You do have to find the best method to learn, spending your time and money to get the right skills you need to get the job, career and/or business you want.

When you have taken the time to plan for your future, and have decided what you want to "be," you need to spend some time figuring out what you can afford. Research and planning is important.

But as you consider what you have available to spend on education, know that the word afford can be very misleading. The questions to ask yourself should concentrate on the issues of what you can afford currently and at what expense to your future.

The truth is many people struggle to pay tuition, have to work part-time and/or incur huge amounts of debt. This is not my definition of the word *afford*. Instead, think of *afford* as equal to *return on investment*. For every dollar you spend, calculate what return you'll get over time, and how long the payback period will last—that is, determine how long it will take for the investment to pay for itself, and then start adding to your total net worth.

Many college graduates are finding out that not only did college take four or more years out of their earning life, but it extended the timeline for other goals as well.

Women, for example, who would like to have a family, find that they have to delay having children because they need to spend time advancing their careers and making enough money to pay off student loans. Another example would be those people who are interested in buying a home but can't save for a down payment or build a good credit rating because they're mired in student loan debt.

Struggling to make college possible when it might not be necessary is a lousy investment. You need to find solutions that allow you to reach your goals, but you need to make sure your investment is equal to your payout. Ask yourself the following questions:

- What are you really passionate about versus what you or others say you should do?

- Is a college education really mandatory, given your career goals?

- Will that college education really get you the job you want when you graduate?

- Can you afford a college that will provide you with the education you need?

- Will the job you get pay enough to allow you to live comfortably and pay back your student loans?

- Will you end up jeopardizing your grades or even continued enrollment because of a part-time job?

The answers to these questions may change over time, and you have to be realistic. For instance, right now, you may be passionate about sitting at home on the couch, eating potato chips, drinking beer, and playing video games. It is unlikely that someone will pay you for this.

Do you have time to invest in your education? What are your priorities in life?

> The average American spends 158.8 hours per month watching television, 25.5 hours using the Internet, 4.5 hours watching video on mobile phones, and 2 hours playing the video game "Angry Birds."[5] What if you went against the grain of our couch-potato culture and spent that time learning skills to advance your success?

The answer to these questions will help you determine whether college is worth the investment for you.

If you are planning on going into debt to get an education that results in getting you a job that won't pay you enough to really get ahead, are you better off? Think about it.

It is important to evaluate your investments. *Forbes* magazine compared the theoretical monetary return on investment for both high school students and college graduates.

If high school graduates were to invest around $144,000, which they would have spent for college, in municipal bonds that pay 5 percent, they would have saved more than $500,000 by the time they reach their mid-30s. This is far more than the average college graduate would earn in the same time period.[6] It is also more than 80 percent of Americans have in total net worth today.

5 *Audacious Birds*, by Nicole Perlroth, *Forbes* magazine, July 18, 2011.
6 "Five Reasons To Skip College" by *Forbes* Staff, April, 18, 2006, www.forbes.com.

The graduates are not without return on their investment; they end up with a degree, but they will be without the money they could have earned working full-time and creating investments.

THE AVERAGE SALARY OF A COLLEGE GRADUATE

A report by the National Association of Colleges and Employers (NACE)[7] shows that average starting salaries for those with a bachelor's degree were:

- Accounting: $45,656

- Business Administration: $42,048

- Information Systems: $45,724

- Computer Science: $51,035

- Chemical Engineering: $56,335

- History: $32,697

- English: $30,944

- Psychology: $30,218

While most starting salaries for the trades[8] are similar and in some cases much higher, the investment in learning a trade skill can be a small fraction of the average college expense of $144,000.

Median Salaries in the Trades

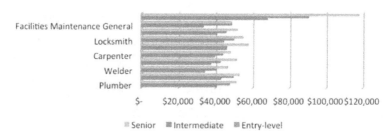

7 National Association of Colleges and Employers (NACE), *Salary Survey*, Summer 2006.
8 Compiled from salary.com, US national averages.

Note that the salaries for most individuals with only a single trade skill, even at the senior level, top out to a median of just under $60,000 a year.

However, as you can see, the facilities maintenance manager with multiple trade skills can make more than $100,000 a year at the senior level. Facilities maintenance at the managerial level requires skills from the seven trades.

Having these seven skill sets puts you in a position to grow your income no matter what career path you choose. It is my belief that the gateway to opportunity lies in knowing multiple trades.

PAYING TOO MUCH FOR TOO LITTLE IN RETURN

More than one in three American families are considered low income and, surprisingly, college is a high-risk investment for this demographic.[9]

"High risk" is not something that should be taken lightly and low income does not mean you are not awarded the same opportunities as everyone else. Attending college for anyone is expensive and most of the time students are not properly prepared for college so they can take advantage of the investment. And, although most colleges offer some financial assistance, this does not guarantee you the ability to get a degree.

Many students are enrolled in a college they cannot afford because of the perception (the college myth) that the more expensive institutions offer the best guarantee for career success. The reality of the situation is that many of these students will require further training after graduation just to get a job. Moreover, many will be

9 americanprogress.org

saddled with debts; they go through all of this, with no assurance that they will get a job in the career of their choice.

According to a UCLA report, the top reason students go to college is to learn about things that interest them.[10] The problem is that college is an expensive place to play around and hope to find a direction that interests you. Celebrities such as Mark Zuckerberg, founder of Facebook; Steve Jobs, founder of Apple; Michael Dell, founder of DELL Computers; and Bill Gates, founder of Microsoft dropped out of college to chase their dreams. College did not provide an environment that fostered their creativity or guided them in their career direction. In fact, they each determined that college was standing in the way of their success.

College does not teach you how to become wealthy or how to start or run a successful business. Most of that knowledge must be acquired outside academic institutions because for the most part they just don't teach that.

The average college professor is broke or has a relatively low net worth. Sometimes college professors can be just plain wrong and not "get it." For example, the college business professor who reviewed Fred Smith's business plan for an express delivery service told him that his plan wouldn't work and gave Smith a C+; he didn't think the business concept was practical. Wisely, Smith ignored him, found some investors, and created a business you may have heard of: FedEx, a multibillion-dollar success story.

There is a saying, "There are people who teach, and then there are people who can do." I have personally found that teaching others is one of the best ways to hone your skills, but when it comes to the

---

10 *American Freshman: Forty-Year Trends 1966–2006,* nasfaa.org

world of pure academics, where very little real, proven experience exists, there is a great deal of truth in that statement.

Choosing a career and figuring out what you enjoy is challenging and college is simply not worth the investment if it is used only for explorative purposes. If you want to find out if your interest in a certain career is founded, get a job in that field and gain first-hand knowledge about it. That is the best way to decide if it is right for you. At the same time you'll earn money and experience for your resume. Sitting in a classroom may help you identify something of interest, but it cannot compare with experiencing it.

As you decide on the career path you want to pursue, you should take some specific courses that will enhance your knowledge. Remember, I am not against learning. Far from it. I believe you commit to a lifetime of learning. You should always keep investing in yourself and in your education. Just do it wisely.

In exploring the right career, ask yourself these key questions:

- Are your career options balanced with your strengths and weaknesses?

- Do they fit your natural aptitudes, preferences, and interests?

- Will your career direction provide you with the financial growth you are looking for?

- What industries are growing and how are you going to be a part of this growth?

There are many components to career planning and your decisions should be thought through carefully. These are questions that will lead to smart decisions.

Every person learns differently and there is no one, uniform system that works for everyone. Many students are unable to find the direction they need in a big college with a vast amount of choice. In addition, there is often a disconnection between the programs available and the reality of the opportunities they provide.

Also, you don't want to make an investment in college if it is not the right environment for you to learn. Work experience is recognized, appreciated, valued, and often weighted as positively as educational degrees, if not more so, for most careers.

As more and more people recognize the college myth for what it is, they become more vocation orientated and develop a greater interest in obtaining skills that quickly and directly translate into a job. As a result, the popularity of technical schools and online learning is rising. People want to and can be in control of their own investment in education and can take a more streamlined approach that can provide positive employment results.

DON'T BOX YOURSELF INTO A CORNER

Today, people seldom choose to work their entire lives in only one occupation. Working in multiple jobs, industries, trades, or for a number of organizations is common. Single-job, single-company stability is not a reality anymore. So you need to pay attention to how you want to make a living, and to what your desired lifestyle is. The Internet has changed the way the world is connected. People today conduct business from the comforts of their own home. And, if you don't desire to work indoors and/or from a cubicle, you can and should consider a career in the trades.

In today's business world, corporations routinely lay off people whenever they need to. There are no guaranteed pensions. There is no security in working for the same company for decades. It is no longer like the old days when you might work for thirty to forty years and get a gold watch and a pension. That era is gone. Self-reliance is the key to survival.

Whether to go to college or not is a decision that should not be taken lightly. As you can see, the costs involved and length of commitment are two primary reasons to consider your return on that investment. It is now more common to find students taking time off to gain work experience, or traveling to figure out a clearer picture of what they want, before they go to college or pursue a particular career.

As we have seen, college is not the only option. You need to realize that there is more than one way to achieve success and prosperity.

Ask yourself:

- Is the cost of college tuition worth the investment?

- Is it a smarter decision to spend the next four years working full-time instead?

- Can work experience provide the same opportunities as a college degree?

It is important to examine what your return on investment will be with a college education. In order to do that you need to start by looking at the most compelling statistic. According to the US Census Bureau, in the year 2000, the average lifetime career earnings of high school graduates totaled $982,880, and the lifetime career earnings of college graduates were $1,827,120. These figures tend to be very misleading. On the surface, it looks as if the college graduate earns double what the high school graduate does. But this is tracking old data, when the demand was high for knowledge workers, and when skilled craftsmen were plentiful. That is certainly not the case today. In fact, the opposite situation now exists and wages in the trades are increasing as a result.

What these figures also don't show is the income potential for entrepreneurs and business owners who seize upon lifetime income opportunities that do not require a college education. In many cases the income levels for these entrepreneurs are much, much higher. After all, most of the millionaires in the USA today are "small" business owners.

> **Success Tip:** It is not just what you earn, but how you earn and spend it. Business owners can legally expense such things as the cars they drive, trips they take, and other legitimate expenses that are related to the business but still benefit the owner. They can also create investments and retirement plans and pay for real estate through the business.

Not all high school graduates will be stuck in jobs without growth potential. Not every individual can be grouped into one statistic. It comes down to you, your own individual ambition, drive, and ability. These are traits that exist because of who you are and strive to be, and not because of your college education.

CHAPTER FOUR

SUCCESS COMES IN MANY FLAVORS

One of the worst mistakes you can make is to choose a career path because you've been told you should choose it, rather than pursue the one that truly interests you. The relationship between a positive, motivated passion and performance in the workplace is widely acknowledged today. This relationship is strongest when your goals are aligned with what you want, what you enjoy doing, and what you are good at.

Unfortunately, many people end up in careers that they do not enjoy and that don't provide them with the lifestyle they truly want to live. Living a life empty of passion and motivation, not your lack of a college degree, is what is going to leave you stuck without opportunity or wealth. You don't want to spend four or more years in college only to find out you've effectively painted yourself into an unhappy, dissatisfied corner.

Motivation is the key to success. If your goals do not excite you to get up in the morning and go at your work with fervor, you need to rethink your objectives.

How do you become motivated? How do you start? An old proverb states: "A journey of 1,000 miles begins with a single step." Goals will help you work toward opportunity and if college is the only direction in which you are looking, you could be missing out. It is a mistake not to recognize or look for alternative sources of opportunity. You have to ask yourself if you are going to college only because of the perception that college graduates have more to offer. Are you going to go to college because that is what you are supposed to do, and if so, who is making the rules?

DOES IT MATTER IF NO ONE ELSE BELIEVES IN YOUR DEFINITION OF SUCCESS? THE ANSWER IS NO. SUCCESS COMES IN MANY FLAVORS.[11]

All that matters is that you believe it and you are motivated, fueled by your faith and passion, to achieve it. Be relentless in your pursuit of life, liberty, and happiness. Find out what it means to you to be in charge of your own destiny. No one else can do it for you, but you have quality help, training, and opportunities available to you. If you seek them out, persistently, you will find them every time, guaranteed, and just right for you.

Realistic thinking is a critical component of success in life and you need to be able to see situations for what they are, not for what people tell you they are. Preconceived beliefs, like those driving the college myth, can cause you to just follow the herd and be less likely to think outside the box. Listen to all the facts, and then form your own opinion.

11 fourhourworkweek.com

THE BIG PICTURE

What is your big picture going to look like, and what path are you going to take, now that you understand that college is not the only option? Getting the most out of your career is achieved when you set realistic goals that are also smart financial choices. There is no point spending more time than necessary to educate yourself in your desired field, and there is no point in losing out on the income potential of those working years.

Write down what you think you are good at and what you think you would like to pursue. Talk to friends and family and gather information about what they think and what experiences they have had. Talk about money and be realistic about what your options are, and what your best plan for financial success is.

Go to: **www.instanttradeskills.com** for a free self-evaluation of your interests and skill sets.

> **Success Tip:** Read and research books and online information regularly. A list of my must-read books for success is available at www.attitradeSchools.com

Interview and/or read about successful people. Most people have someone, or a group of people, that they admire, whether it is a celebrity or an acquaintance. Figure out what you like about them and learn about what they did to get where they are today. It should come as no surprise to learn that many of them are not college graduates. There are multiple paths that can lead to success. The objective is to source information that is interesting and significant to you and your goals. This is a great way to figure out how to achieve your goals and become motivated. Your own research is the key to making decisions that are good for you.

Today you do not need a degree to be successful. As soon as you realize this, a new world of alternative opportunities will present itself. The worst thing you can do is to believe the assumptions driving the college myth and plan your life around the "herd" that could lead to the "slaughter."

Be aware. If you make the decision not to go to college, you will encounter pressure and opposition from others who believe in the college myth.

The myth that college is the best way to secure a successful future is widely believed and people like the idea of a guaranteed success. They are often greatly disappointed.

However, you are an individual with your own drives and needs, and you must have your own game plan. So take a stand. The most effective way to deal with outside pressures is to have your own plan. The last thing you want is to be influenced by others' opinions.

Knowing what you want and what you need to do to get yourself there is the best way to conquer the criticism. Having your own individual game plan shows that you are not willing to go along with what everyone else is doing, and you are self reliant. It also shows that you pay attention to what is important to you and what drives your own personal motivation.

Therefore, whether you are looking to start your own entrepreneurial endeavor, get direct work experience, enroll in online education, or even go to college, when you have a plan, chances are people will be willing to recognize your ambition and provide you with support.[12]

12 "Sure You Should Go to College?" by Marty Nemko, martynemko.com.

Opportunity is a concept that lures you with promises of change and the potential for success, but it is not an opportunity unless it matches your skills, abilities, and ambitions. College is not a great opportunity for everyone, so you need to individualize your life for what is going to make you successful. There will be many times in your life when you fail to understand the significance of opportunities presented to you until they have passed.

How many times in your life have you said, "I should have done it differently"? Your future is not something to gamble with, and the financial impact and uncertainties of the value of college need to be carefully considered. You must have the vision to look past the common college perception and explore all of the other alternatives.

ASK YOURSELF HONESTLY WHOM YOU ARE TRYING TO IMPRESS WITH A COLLEGE DEGREE

A degree is a piece of paper that only has meaning when you can apply it or when you need it as a prerequisite. Employers will not hire you just because you have a college degree; they will hire you because of the other skills and experience that you have to offer. As you have learned, there are many avenues that do not include a college degree as a prerequisite for success. It is important that you be true to yourself and honest about your choices.

In making a choice about college, you have to ask yourself whether college teaches you the skills you need to be successful and make money. Ask yourself whether, in addition to teaching core vocational skills, college teaches you:

- how to recognize opportunity

- how to make money and create wealth

CHAPTER FIVE

WHO WANTS TO BE A MILLIONAIRE?

Approximately 4,300,000 millionaires live in the USA today, but where are they all hidden?

Most millionaires live in average neighborhoods. They do not inherit their money, but earn it in small businesses and entrepreneurial ventures. Of the 300,000 neighborhoods in the USA, more than half of them have at least one millionaire.

While their individual paths to wealth vary, all millionaires share some common characteristics: their ability to save and accumulate wealth, their strong work ethic, and their willingness to take educated financial risks to grow their wealth. Two-thirds of them are business owners and entrepreneurs.

A DEGREE DOES NOT EQUAL ENTREPRENEURIAL SUCCESS

Young entrepreneurs create new successful ventures every day and you can too.

The Internet and other technologies allow almost everybody the chance to launch an online business, or start a business and promote its success worldwide.

Many argue that the ease of starting a new business on the web has created false hopes for young people and discredits the value of education. The truth is the success of a web-based business requires the same genetic make-up as that of any other business. The success or failure still depends on a person's abilities, and the Internet is simply a media that has created increased opportunity for prospective entrepreneurs.

> Successful people who don't go to college make up for their lack of a degree with "tenacity, brains, guts, and strong business sense." (Kate Lorenz)[13]

Here are a few entrepreneurial success stories to prove it.

Richard Branson, founder of The Virgin Group, which is made up of 350 companies, does not have a college degree. Today he is the chairman of the Virgin Group, which includes Virgin Atlantic megastores and hotels.

Barry Diller, the chairman of Expedia and CEO of IAC/Inter-ActiveCorp, dropped out of UCLA after one semester and started his career in the mailroom of the William Morris Agency. At age thirty-two, he was the president of Paramount Pictures.

Rachael Ray, Emmy-winning TV personality, began her career in Macy's department store at the candy counter and moved her way into a management position in the fresh foods department. She eventually started teaching classes, "Thirty-Minute Meals," that grew in popularity, and she was featured on the evening news. From there she was picked up by the Food Network.

13 Success Without a College Degree? by Kate Lorenz, careerbuilder.com, Sept. 24, 2007.

Peter Jennings, ABC's broadcast journalist, attended Carleton University and quickly dropped out. From there he went on to a job at the Royal Bank of Canada and pursued his passion for acting on the side. At the age of twenty-one, Jennings entered broadcasting in an entry-level position at a local radio station. His career flourished and today he is one of television's most famous journalists.

Larry Ellison, co-founder of Oracle, and a multibillionaire, was a self-taught computer programmer who dropped out of college and started a freelance career.

Simon Cowell, another college dropout, started his career in the mailroom of EMI Music. He is best known as a judge on *American Idol*. He also launched several ventures including promotions companies and Syco Music Publishing.

John Simplot, inventor of the frozen French fry dropped out of eighth grade and worked on a farm before branching out into manufacturing. His company provides all the potatoes for McDonald's French fries. He was a billionaire and a major stockholder of Micron Technologies.

Tom Monaghan, founder of Domino's Pizza franchise, dropped out of the University of Michigan and moved to Chicago. The real magic happened when he became interested in the pizza business. With a $900 loan, a plan to fill a need he saw in the marketplace (delivery in thirty minutes or less), and some courage, he created a pizza empire he sold for hundreds of millions of dollars.

Dave Thomas, founder of Wendy's, was a high school dropout. His real success came from salvaging failing KFC restaurant chains. From there he became an entrepreneur and opened Wendy's Old Fashioned Hamburgers, which is now the third most successful burger chain in America.

Wayne Huizenga, another college dropout, turned a used garbage truck into a trash hauling operation. Today he is now a waste management business success and owner of the Miami Dolphins Stadium.

These highly successful individuals skipped or dropped out of college to chase their dreams and created businesses and identities that are known throughout the world. There is absolutely no reason why you cannot do the same. It's important to note that, even though all these people pursued very different businesses, the one thing all of these entrepreneurs had in common is that they did what was right for them and they did it well.

The point is that success doesn't necessarily follow the conventional path, and when you have drive and ambition, you can get to where you want to be. There is no right or wrong way to become a success; there is only your way.

You cannot underestimate the value of possessing skills that are in demand in the marketplace. Even though there is an implied link between a college education and future promotion, it is not to say that an individual without a degree will not have the same or even greater odds of success. You need to increase your skills and abilities in a way that will directly affect your career interests. There are many employers who have hired numerous individuals and never asked to see their degree. Most importantly, employers want to find out what you know and how you know it.

WHAT DOES IT TAKE TO JOIN THE 1 PERCENT OF THE US POPULATION WHO ARE MILLIONAIRES?

Wealth is accumulated by hard work, skill, knowledge, smart investment strategies, and ambition.[14]

14 *The Millionaire Next Door: The Surprising Secrets of America's Wealthy,* by Thomas J. Stanley and William D. Danko, Taylor Trade Publishing (1996).

> ### Which 1 Percent Will You Be?
> It is interesting to me to hear that 1 percent of the people in the USA are millionaires and it was recently reported that 1 percent of the population of the USA are in prison. What do you think the difference is? I personally believe that the difference is about being aware of the opportunities in life, then making choices and accepting personal responsibility for those choices and their outcomes.
>
> -Thomas Stanley[15]

Yes, you too can become a millionaire if you follow this relatively simple but proven formula:

1. As quickly as possible, learn a trade or profession that will enable you to get a high-paying job, or, better yet, own a business.

2. Discover what ignites your unique interest, motivation, and/or passion, not focused on following the masses, but leading them.

3. Find a particular need in the marketplace, related to your interests and passion, and fill it.

4. Marry and stay married.

5. Live below your means, spending less than you make.

6. Invest the surplus income from your job or business in positive cash-flowing real estate or other growth investments, held for the long term: ten to twenty-plus years.

7. Continue to invest in your personal growth and education.

15 Ibid.

8. Be a life-long learner, investing in your trade, business, and financial education.

That's it. The vast majority of wealthy people in the USA have successfully followed this simple formula for generations.

MILLIONAIRE MYTHS REVEALED

So again, do you want to be a millionaire? This may seem to be a ridiculous question. The obvious answer for most would be, "Yes, but I couldn't be one without winning the lottery," or "Yes, but they still had some sort of genius and/or dumb luck." First, you need to understand the difference between the Hollywood millionaire and the real millionaire. The truth is that becoming a millionaire is not impossible; in fact, people like you do it every day.

- Do you have what it takes to be a millionaire?

- Do you spend less than you earn?

People who buy a new car every few years, always have the latest gadgets, and live in flashy neighborhoods are probably not really rich. They probably want to appear rich, and feel rich, but chances are they are not millionaires.

As we often see in the news, Hollywood millionaires or sports stars are frequently broke later in life no matter how much money flowed through their hands.

According to an interview with Thomas J. Stanley, coauthor of the book, *The Millionaire Next Door: The Surprising Secrets of America's Wealthy,* the truly wealthy do not live this way. Most live in average neighborhoods and do not inherit their money but earn it in entrepreneurial business ventures. Stanley describes the characteristics of a millionaire as an ability to accumulate wealth, a strong work ethic, and what he or she does for a living. The truth is that millionaires take risks and two thirds of them are entrepreneurs.

As an entrepreneur, you are the boss and your success or failures are your own. It is this career path that forces business owners to gain a realistic appreciation for money as a tool and what is required to make it, keep it, and have it grow. People who become rich are concerned with investment and long-term financial planning. You need to learn how to make money and save money efficiently. Then focus on wealth creation and investment.

According to Stanley, the majority of students graduating from top US MBA schools don't know what the most profitable businesses are in the country. Parents send their children to college in the hope that education will provide them with a life that is more financially stable and less stressful than theirs. The truth is that today, kids are working harder for less, and are on the wrong path for long-term net worth growth. As a result, they are stressed and financially unstable.

WHAT ARE THE MOST PROFITABLE BUSINESSES IN THE COUNTRY?

Stanley concludes that the majority of them are in the low-tech trades, the types of industry that people do not go to college for. Examples would be construction, dry cleaning, transportation, and maintenance.

The problem is that that these types of industry are perceived to be low-paying occupations. If this silly social stigma deters you from making realistic and profitable choices, you need to pay attention to what is real, not what others perceive to be real.

Stanley's book supports the theory that no one gets rich working for someone else. Self-employment is a journey that provides challenges that force you to be more concerned with money. Below is a description of a typical American millionaire today.

> Profile of Typical Millionaires
>
> Business owners, probably in a low-tech business;
> Live in houses ranging in price from $145,000 to $350,000 with the average being $278,000;
>
> 97 percent of them are homeowners and have occupied the same home for more than twenty years;
>
> Drive regular cars. not flashy or expensive imports;
>
> One in five are retired; two-thirds are self-employed;
>
> Occupations are typically perceived as dull or typical: trade contractors, farmers, dry cleaners, exterminators, and so on;
>
> Live on less than 7 percent of their total wealth;
>
> 80 percent of them are first-generation affluent (self-made);
>
> Two-thirds of them work forty-five- to fifty-hour weeks;
>
> 20 percent of their household wealth is invested in stocks, mutual funds, and real estate.[16]

The reality is that most millionaires are first-generation rich. Only 19 percent have received income or wealth from a trust fund, and less than 20 percent have inherited 10 percent or more of their wealth.[17] This means you can become wealthy too.

There is something to be said about the difference between appearing wealthy and actually being wealthy. There is also something to be said about understanding what makes you happy and identify-

16 "Under the Affluence," interview with Thomas J. Stanley, coauthor of *The Millionaire Next Door: The Surprising Secrets of America's Wealthy* by Lorayne Fiorillo, entrepreneur. com, May 1999

17 *The Millionaire Next Door: The Surprising Secrets of America's Wealthy* by Thomas J. Stanley and William D. Danko, Taylor Trade Publishing (1996).

ing your picture of success. Wealth, whether real or not, does not equal happiness.

So, start looking at life as a sea of opportunity that you can take advantage of instead of following a bunch of predefined paths. There is certainly more than one path you can take, and as I have demonstrated, contrary to popular perception, the college path does not always lead to success.

Accumulators of wealth spend time and money learning and understanding how to invest. Stanley explains that high-income individuals who accumulate wealth are significantly less likely to hold a graduate, law, or medical degree than those with a high income who never seem to get truly wealthy—although they may look that way.

When interviewed for Stanley's surveys, millionaires typically indicated that they were business owners with "some college" or no degree. He attributes this to the fact that these types of people with high incomes had a head start making and investing money while doctors and lawyers spent many years in college and then spent the next several decades paying off student loans.

It is important to start investing money early when you are looking to accumulate wealth. Wealth and success is not about luck and it is rarely from inheritance. This statistic demonstrates that every person has the potential for wealth. This statistic does not discriminate between a college graduate and a high school graduate. According to Stanley, there are seven main characteristics of wealthy people.

> ### Characteristics of Wealthy People[18]
>
> Wealthy people live below their means.
>
> Wealthy people spend their time and energy focused on building wealth.
>
> Wealthy people place more importance on financial independence than social status.
>
> Wealthy people do not receive ongoing assistance from their parents.
>
> Wealthy people's adult children are financially self-sufficient because their parents teach them to be.
>
> Wealthy people are proficient in targeting potential marketing or business opportunities.
>
> Wealthy people choose the right occupation or business.

LEARNING A TRADE OR SKILL EARLY ON IS THE FIRST PART OF THE SUCCESS EQUATION

To become independent and self-reliant it is important to understand how and why something works the way it does.

Technical training in a trade teaches you how to do a particular job as well as understand why the job is done a certain way. Learn these core skills early on, and then build additional skills.

To be successful as a business owner or entrepreneur you'll also need to learn the skills of sales, marketing, personal development, and money management. Why? This is the entire package that not only jump-starts your success, but most importantly, allows you to create further opportunity that leads to wealth.

Learning a trade also gives you the option of earning a significant income or creating your own business if you so choose. You can

18 *The Millionaire Next Door: The Surprising Secrets of America's Wealthy* by Thomas J. Stanley and William D. Danko, Taylor Trade Publishing (1996).

achieve success and become comfortably wealthy working in a high-paying job in the trades.

But it is not just about making money; what you do with your money counts as well. Money is not just made by business people. Welders, contractors, exterminators, plumbers, dry cleaners, and carpenters, just to name a few, can also create significant wealth.

CHAPTER SIX

MAKING SUCCESS HAPPEN, EVEN WHEN YOU FAIL

Too many people believe that career success is outside of their control, and too much emphasis is put on educational status. There is a fine line between sacrifice and insanity, and you need to be sure you are not sacrificing your time and money on false promises. You need to create a plan that will provide you with your own individual opportunities. Be careful not to group yourself with the masses.

FEAR OF FAILURE

One of the biggest barriers holding people back in life is the fear of failure—and the fear of it can be big, even bigger than you think you can handle. But try to look at that fear as unbridled passion that just needs a direction. Think of it as motivational energy that needs a positive channel to plug into. Fear, at first is normal and to your advantage because it causes the hyper vigilance you need to discover and take the right action. And you will fail some battles, but not the overall victory. Never give up and never give in to the fear of failure.

I am very successful. Part of the reason that I am is that I, like other entrepreneurs, am not afraid to fail. In fact, if I am going to fail, I want to do so quickly so that I can learn from that experience, minimize my losses, recalibrate, and move forward again.

You will find that most of the people you think of as successful have "failed" numerous times. Donald Trump "failed" in the early 1990s when he was more than $900 million in debt and practically bankrupt. What if he had quit then? He is now a billionaire and his name is world famous.

What I have found is that you need to acquire the attitude: "I am going to try and then fail, forward, fast."

When you understand this concept you will become really powerful at creating successful outcomes.

What I mean by "fail, forward, fast" is that you must learn as much as you can about a situation or opportunity and do so rapidly. Choose the path that appears to be the best based on the information you have. Then, move quickly on it.

If you give yourself the freedom to "fail" and let go of any pride and ego, often the momentum that you develop, along with the knowledge and experience you acquire from the "failed" efforts, will carry you toward success.

Pursued in this fashion, many of your efforts will become great successes, and you will benefit from having tried while others are stuck doing nothing simply because of their fear of failure. Be willing to risk, fail, and succeed. I guarantee you will survive it, with a lot more skill and character—and even better, you'll prosper.

Thomas Edison, the famous inventor, was asked about how it felt to have more than a thousand experiments fail when he was trying to invent the light bulb. He replied, "I didn't fail a thousand times; I simply found a thousand ways that it didn't work." He also said, "If you want to increase your success rate, double your failure rate." What kind of world would we be living in if Mr. Edison had quit at 999 attempts? You would be reading this by candlelight.

To succeed: adopt "fail, forward, fast" as one of your core principles. Merely grasping this concept and holding it as your own will greatly help to reduce or even eliminate your fears and push you toward success.

Failure is part of the learning process. If you were to succeed at everything you tried, why would you try to improve? Chances are, if you are always successful, you are not taking big enough risks and pushing your limits for success. Failure is a word that is completely misunderstood. Most of all, it simply means, "I didn't achieve the desired results." It is all about how you perceive the experience.

Like Edison, most millionaires will tell you that you have to be willing to risk failure before you fast-forward and succeed. In fact, it is the most effective way to test your limits. If you are going to become wealthy, you cannot be afraid to fail and you cannot become discouraged. Playing it safe did not propel anyone into the top 1 percent of wealth in America. It took innovation, risk, and perseverance.

DARE TO STAND OUT

When employers look at a pool of candidates they are not looking for uniformity; they are looking for an individual who stands out. When you interview for a position, you need to be able to show your innovation and creativity, which will separate you from the rest of the pack.

Success Tip: Bring examples of your work or accomplishments with you to an interview if they are applicable in anyway.

Your individual level of desire to succeed is the most important contribution to your performance and the essential ingredient that allows you to continue to reach your full potential. When you force yourself into a situation that does not match your desire, goals, or strengths, you are essentially forcing yourself to be someone you are not. This is not a recipe for success; it is a path of self-destruction. College simply is not a match for every individual's personal style.

You need to figure out what you want to achieve, set your goals, and make smart decisions about how to reach them. Then become relentless. There will be failures along the way. Yet, if you are not able to persevere and continue to take risks throughout your life, you will not be able to take advantage of all the opportunities that lead to personal success.

How dedicated are you to becoming successful and wealthy? Many people say they want it, but never develop the will and determination to create and maintain their drive. How are you going to find your drive? It starts by choosing the right training in skills that are aligned with your goals and that you are personally excited to learn.

It is not an easy process to figure out exactly what you are passionate about and what goals equate with your definition of success. Perhaps you already know what you want to do for a career, but you think it is outside your reach. Trust me it is not.

One of the biggest problems people have is not taking the time to research what their options are. Don't assume you cannot gain the skills and experience needed for a particular career because you cannot afford college or you do not have the prerequisites to enter college. Today there are many different ways to gain both the education and work experience required to achieve your goals.

> **Success Tip:** Why not learn trade skills fast and travel the world? What if you could learn several different trades for about the same cost as a year of college, and in one-quarter of the time conventional methods take? You could spend the next three years traveling the world, getting real-life experience, and still be ahead financially. To find out more, go to www.instanttradeskills.com

It is important that you think in terms of what you enjoy and what kind of lifestyle you are looking to have. Do not think in terms of a specific career if you are undecided. Instead, start by making a list of skills and activities that you like to do. Beginning the brainstorming process is the first step to creating a clearer picture of your future.

Decisions can seem final, but you need to consistently remind yourself they are not. What you are doing is creating guidelines for yourself and figuring out your options for reaching your goals. You may find along the way that what you thought you would like is not what you want and you may go in a new direction. The most important point is to gain skills, start your career, and earn a living. Whatever you discover along the way will be an added bonus.

CHAPTER SEVEN

THE TRADES: AN ALTERNATIVE ROUTE TO WEALTH

Today, jobs and businesses in the skilled-trade industries are providing big earning potential. Demand for skilled labor is increasing with business opportunities and room to grow.

When you choose a trade, essentially you create a foundation for lifelong success. Learning a trade isn't just about earning money; it is really about becoming self-reliant, personally powerful, and confident by acquiring skills that provide you with the ability to create income and personal freedom. These are always-in-demand skills that match opportunities in the marketplace. Possessing multiple trade skills gives you the freedom to make your own choices.

It is often best to learn several related trades. This type of cross-training is incredibly valuable because it provides you with insights that others lack in this era of extreme overspecialization.

For example, many draftsmen with computer-aided design (CAD/CAM) skills have never machined a part, constructed a building, or fabricated a metal structure, but they create blueprints for these very things. Think about how much better off they would be if they had the practical experience of making something.

Possessing trade knowledge and experience brings a whole new level of understanding and eliminates mistakes in product design. So, no matter what career you ultimately choose, possessing a series of trade skills is an investment in yourself that will pay off over a lifetime.

Be a life-long learner, not a one-trick pony. You will derive far more satisfaction from life by continuing to learn and you'll become much more valuable in the process. In fact, a person with multiple trade skills and the right mindset is virtually worry-free when it comes to earning an income.

Learning an in-demand trade can be a stepping stone to business ownership for those who are willing to take the necessary risks associated with owning a business. Although it's not for everyone, business ownership is still the surest path to becoming rich. Learning a trade and leveraging it into a business is the swiftest and surest way to success. True, not all businesses succeed. Most fail, but every area of life contains an element of risk.

Unfortunately, many of the professions that can lead to wealth and don't require a college degree are not widely publicized. Many low-tech trade businesses have greater earning potential than many professions considered to be highly paid.

People who are financially successful are usually personally successful. People who spend time pursuing what they enjoy achieve better balance in their lives and personal fulfillment. You need to do a self-evaluation to identify your professional and personal interests. You must do your homework to figure out how to achieve your goals.

Self-examination will help you narrow down a career direction that is compatible with who you are and what you want to be. You should think about the hours you want to work and what type of environment you want to work in. In order to do this, you have to ask yourself tough questions. You don't have to know the answers right away, but asking such questions will start the brainstorming process.

The purpose of self-examination is not to create a concrete path, but to create self-awareness. The worst mistake is making a decision without any consideration. This process is not easy and using others to help can be effective.

Success Tip: One of the best ways to figure out your desired career direction is through research. A lot of information exists out there to educate you on potential opportunities and job market statistics. Personality testing is available to highlight your strengths and weaknesses.

CHAPTER EIGHT

WORK EDUCATION THAT CAN WORK FOR YOU

> Work education is a practice that emphasizes the development of knowledge, skills and attitudes as it relates to a student's future participation within the economic sector of one's community and nation.[19]

There is no substitute for hands-on experience when you do your research on career choices, and there are many ways to gain work experience, both paid and nonpaid. Consider an internship or an apprenticeship that allows you to work in the real world in the profession of your interest.

The last thing you want to do is invest in education for a career you do not even know for certain you will like. An internship or apprenticeship gives you a chance to try before you buy. Generally, the hours for this type of work are somewhat flexible so you can fit it into your schedule.

19 *Learning Work: A Critical Pedagogy of Work Education* by Roger I. Simon, Don Dippo and Arleen Schenke, Greenwood Publishing Group , April 1991.

The purpose of an internship or apprenticeship is to provide you with real-life work experience and the resources to start building a network of contacts for future opportunities. The end result is that you gain an accurate picture of what your day-to-day work life will be like and can make decisions based on experience.

An internship or job in your chosen field helps you develop your resume and makes you a more competitive candidate in the marketplace. Finding a job is not easy, even if you have a college degree, but an apprenticeship or part-time work can sometimes lead to a full-time opportunity.

Finding an internship or a job is similar; you need to do your research and persevere. There are many online career sites and employment centers where you can gather information about various job opportunities.

WHAT ELSE ARE EMPLOYERS LOOKING FOR?

The ability to clearly communicate is one of the top skills employers look for in a new employee. Examples are: learning how to ask an intelligent question, accurately reporting a situation or current status of a project, and being able to confirm that you understand what you are being asked to do. While these seem simple, trust me, most employees do a very poor job of communicating clearly and accurately.

Employers are also looking at your levels of personal motivation, ability to do teamwork, and analytical and leadership skills.[20]

These skills are certainly attainable through avenues other than attending college. Employers look at what you have accomplished.

---

20 "What Do Employers Really Want? Top Skills and Values Employers Seek from Job-Seekers," by Randall S. Hansen, Ph.D., and Katharine Hansen, Ph.D., www.quintcareers.com.

Whether it is employment, volunteering, or extracurricular work, they look at what you have been involved in and the specific skills you have developed. It's no longer a question of a high college GPA. "Soft skills" are often important to employers, and it is real-life experience that helps you develop them.

A resume is not just about listing education and job experience. Employers look for traits in a candidate such as willingness to learn, problem solving abilities, and initiative. These are skills that most employers feel cannot be taught in the classroom and have to do with individual attitude and character.

Employers want to hire people who have learned these soft skills, and they want to hear examples of how and where they were developed. Individuals who have learned real trade skills, where problem solving is an everyday part of life, often develop and excel at these highly desired soft skills as well.

It is more important to develop real trade skills and social and interpersonal communications skills than it is to get a college degree.

Here's a little secret: when interviewing potential employees, employers really only want to know three things:

1. What do you know?

2. What have you done (experience)?

3. What can you do for me?

That's it. Frankly, everything else is largely irrelevant. I have sat across the table interviewing numerous potential employees, and what I always think as I sit there is, "What do you know, what have you done, what can you do for me?"

If the answers aren't clear, I keep looking. A college graduate who is not able to get through the interviewing process and articulate his or her strengths will have a tough time finding a job. Your education should incorporate a hands-on approach that not only allows you to learn about something in theory but also teaches you how to do it in the real world.

The best technical schools incorporate both the theoretical and practical as well as valuable job skills development so you are able to sell yourself to an employer.

Specialized applied learning brings relevance to your education. College, on the other hand, requires you to take a variety of courses that do not have anything to do with what you will be doing in your job.

Education should be about building your professional qualifications, and although a degree indicates that you have the ability to learn, it does not guarantee to an employer, the one who pays you money, that you have the skills to do a particular job.

There is nothing taught at a four-year college that cannot be learned somewhere else for less money and in a shorter amount of time.

You do not need to learn about eighteenth-century art to become an entrepreneur or work as a trade contractor. So unless it personally interests you, why would you study it?

WHY NETWORKING IS MORE IMPORTANT THAN A DEGREE

Never forget that the people you meet and the references you receive will contribute more to your continued success than a degree. References are invaluable and necessary for many job applications. Every work opportunity gives you the chance to do a great job and make a great impression.

If you can show a potential employer that you are a hard-working and responsible individual, you have given yourself a significant step up on your competition.

The truth is that even college graduates struggle with career direction and finding opportunities. In addition to having real world, in-demand trade skills, networking has become one of the biggest factors involved in landing a great job. A personal recommendation often carries more weight than your credentials.

A personal reference will get you through the door, so you need to make sure that you put yourself out there. Immerse yourself in activities that will lead you to future opportunity. Companies would much prefer to hire a person who comes with a personal recommendation than a candidate without one.

It is important that, as a candidate, you bring the proper skill set to the table. So if you focus on becoming involved in a company that supports your major area of interest and network to get onboard, you'll have a much greater chance of creating your own opportunities than those who just shop for a job and rely on their paper degree.

CHAPTER NINE

WHO SUCCEEDS IN TECHNICAL AND/ OR TRADE SCHOOLS AND WHY?

The traditional description of a college candidate is identical to the description of someone who has the potential to learn a trade.

If those people were to learn a trade instead of going to college, they would learn faster with the flexibility to learn at their own pace, and they would do so at a lower cost.

Self-motivated students are not necessarily well suited for a classroom environment anyway because most of the time they are too advanced and would benefit better from being in control of their own learning experiences. Einstein, for example, was initially thought to be slow because he didn't do well in the traditional, structured classroom. In actuality, he was bored.

One of the main differences between a four-year college and technical school is that the focus is on developing exclusively and specifically the skills needed to succeed in a particular job or jobs.

Technical schools are dedicated to aligning their curricula with the real-world needs of current job trends and therefore offer classes that teach skills that are in demand. As such, they are often very vocationally focused and much more practical in their approach than academic institutions.

Technical schools no longer solely focus on upgrading skills or continuing education. Today they directly attract high school students looking to quickly gain hands-on training for faster and higher-paying job placement.

The flexibility of technical schools has opened doors to a variety of demographic profiles including high school grads, those who did not graduate from high school, former military personnel, the unemployed, those retraining after job loss, employees seeking to increase their skills, and retirees wanting to produce additional income, all because they can attend classes virtually in their own time. Also, the ability to study and work at the same time is a financial necessity for many people with families.

> **Success Tip:** Your success will most likely be reflected by the five people you spend the most time with. Think about those you hang around with. If they are not successful, you may want to find some new friends.

Economist Robert Reischauer believes that students who are driven are more likely to go to college, but he attributes their success after college to their drive and not their formal education.[21]

---

21 "Five Reasons To Skip College" by *Forbes* staff, forbes.com, April 18, 2006.

When you have the natural ability and drive for success, it makes more sense to spend less time on education and more time earning money.

ARE YOU SMART?

The belief that a college dropout, or someone who didn't attend college at all, lacks ambition and isn't smart is unfounded.

According to the Bureau of Economic Research, the income potential of high-school dropouts has nothing to do with education.[22] From this you can conclude that it is a person's inherent ability and level of desire to succeed, which creates success with or without a college degree.

Between 2005 and 2007, the University of California at Los Angeles conducted a nationwide survey titled *Your First College Year*. The survey concluded that only 16.4 percent of students were satisfied with the overall quality of instruction they received and 28.2 percent were neutral, dissatisfied, or very dissatisfied. They did a follow up study for seniors and they found that 37 percent were "frequently bored in class," which is an increase of 27.5 percent of the freshman year statistic.[23]

Further, according to a survey completed by Collegegrad.com, which included 2,350 recent college graduates in 2004 (the most recent US economic boom), 18 percent of the participants were not working in jobs that required a college degree.

Also, according to Marty Nemko, PhD, who specializes in the evaluation of education at the University of California, Berkeley, the

22 ibid
23 "We Send Too Many Students to College" by Marty Nemko, MartyNemko.com.

number of underemployed college graduates in today's declining economy is most likely much, much higher.

Marty also questions whether it is proper for counselors to encourage weak high school students to seek college admission. Many below-average students attend college mostly to prove they can do it, and they struggle throughout their courses or drop out discouraged. Nemko believes certain students should be encouraged to pursue other options that will better accommodate their learning styles and increase the success of their results.[24]

In the past decade an incredible boom of entrepreneurship has sprung up around the world. Entrepreneurs are smart, self-made individuals. The profile of an entrepreneur has changed drastically, has become more diverse, and includes nearly every demographic.

Starting a new business involves fewer risks than in the past, and it is easier for you to start a business without quitting your job. People are finding employment solutions that concentrate on their strengths, abilities, and lifestyle. The truth is you do not have to work for someone else and, as small businesses around the country continue to flourish, more and more people are jumping onboard.

---

24   "Higher Education: America's Most Overrated Product" by Marty Nemko, MartyNemko.com.

CHAPTER TEN

WHAT DOES CREATING SUCCESS AND THE RIGHT CAREER DIRECTION MEAN TO YOU?

S uccess involves more than knowing all the answers. More importantly, success starts with asking the right questions. Let's begin with the basics of what success means.

What would you consider a good income? The answer to this can be different for each individual because everyone has varied needs, wants, and interests. For all of us, though, a good income is one that will allow us to live our preferred lifestyle.

What level of income do you need to accomplish your goals? Income will allow you to:

1. Pay for needs

2. Pay for wants

3. Invest surplus to create passive income

Beyond these simple numbers, the success equation also includes the ideal of security. So you have to ask yourself if working for someone else guarantees your security. The truth is job security is no longer a reality. Between 70,000 and 80,000 corporate employees are laid off each month.[25] So how do you create job security in your success equation?

WILL THAT COLLEGE EDUCATION CREATE JOB SECURITY?

A college education does not guarantee you a corporate position and it does not guarantee you security and wealth. Face it. In today's economy you need to create your own financial security by making yourself a valuable individual through specific skills sets you have acquired.

DO YOU EXPECT TO BE AN ENTREPRENEUR AT SOME POINT IN YOUR LIFE?

When this question was asked of students, more than 66 percent said yes. This survey found that males are more likely to take the leap with 74 percent setting their sights on entrepreneurship versus 59 percent of their female peers, says Alvin Rohrs, SIFE president and CEO.[26]

IS BECOMING AN ENTREPRENEUR LESS RISKY AND MORE REWARDING THAN GETTING A COLLEGE DEGREE?

It used to be that any form of entrepreneurship was considered risky and you were much better off getting an education and a job with a reputable firm. Today there are risks involved in both. It comes down to considering where you are most likely to succeed. The only risk you should avoid is not considering your options.

---

25 "Everyone wants to start a business" by Phaedra Hise, money.cnn.com, February 1, 2007.
26 SIFE survey, fall 2002, sife.org.

> Entrepreneurs are more innovative than large corporate organizations and more likely to be involved in the community, donate to charity, and join appointed boards. As small business grows, so will the country's innovation.[27]

Small business today is more forgiving when it comes to the risks. Technology has opened up the marketplace and created a small business platform for many new creative ideas.

However, becoming an entrepreneur still involves risk. In fact, over half of all entrepreneurs fail the first time out, but many subsequently succeed after multiple attempts. How driven are you to succeed?

Outside factors are sometimes responsible for failure, but failure is not without personal blame. Your ability to foster ambition and drive is the most important factor for success. You need to have the confidence to succeed regardless of the path you choose and you need to be accountable for your own performance. You are in control of many of the factors that will lead to your success.

WHAT ARE YOUR EXPECTATIONS OF YOURSELF? ARE THEY REALISTIC?

Perhaps you are unrealistic about what you are trying to achieve or perhaps you are not ambitious enough. Ask yourself these tough questions:

- What specifically is holding you back?

- What is the source of your motivation?

- Are you ready to be a success even if it means a change in direction that might include giving up friends, habits, and unprofitable behaviors?

27 "Everyone wants to start a business" by Phaedra Hise, money.cnn.com, February 1, 2007.

You cannot be afraid to make a change. For instance, your college experience does not prevent you from starting over again.

The worst thing you can do is stay stagnant when something is clearly not working. As the saying goes, when you find yourself in a hole, quit digging. Sometimes changing your career is what you need. Changing careers does not mean that you failed at the first one. Poor choices do not always have to be permanent.

For every risk there is a benefit, and there really is nothing worth having in life that is risk-free. There are many benefits of working for yourself: you get to choose your own lifestyle (eventually), there can be endless earning potential, you gain a valuable knowledge base that you can't get from a corporate environment, and you have control.

Risk is subjective, and for many who have jobs they dislike, with no guarantee of job security, the risk is much bigger. The truth is that most successful people like what they do.

When you are uncertain about your career direction, you will miss opportunities to get the right training and take important steps, which produces unnecessary stress and anxiety. Stress and anxiety about your future can create negative thought patterns that will affect your ambition and drive. Don't let them.

When you realize there are many options out there besides college, you will no longer lack the confidence to discover your potential. Many students' biggest source of stress is indecision, which is compounded by the high investment costs of a college education. For many it is not a question of whether they should go; it is a question of having to go and needing to figure out how to make it happen at all costs. This is not a productive way to look at your future.

There are many reasons for choosing the wrong career path, which is usually attributed to a lack of confidence or a lack of knowledge about the opportunities available. Moreover, people often choose careers they do not want due to external influences, not personal aspirations. This is unfortunately the same reason many people go to college: because they think they have to.

Finding the right career direction, choosing the right educational program, and identifying opportunity is not easy, but it is worth the effort. To reach your full career potential, you need to choose what is best for you, and you can't do that until you learn the facts about how to get the job you want and accumulate wealth.

Intellectual stimulation is not exclusively satisfied or developed in an educational institution. In fact, for many, real-life experience in which they can see the results of what they are learning is more effective.

Every individual learns differently and depending on the skill set you are trying to develop, you need to decide which environment is right for your learning needs. Which environment is going to make you the best that you can be and which environment makes sense for the goals that you have set?

CHAPTER ELEVEN

THE DISTANCE LEARNING ALTERNATIVE

G ood news! You don't have to attend a bricks-and-mortar conventional school to get the training you need to succeed. Many new companies offer innovative technology to teach you in record time at a fraction of the cost of conventional schools.

The educational needs of students are changing and according to Mona Westhaver, a founder of Inspiration Software, which specializes in visual learning software, "A revolution is needed in education. Students exist in a world where technology is pervasive, but classroom teaching hasn't basically changed in fifty years."

The educational technology industry is rapidly growing as the need for specialized training increases. People require effective ways to learn skills, including distance learning methods that are fast, flexible, and affordable. A great deal of development and growth has occurred in both technology and technical education. Today those advancements enable you to learn a trade without physical attendance in a classroom and without spending as many years as you would in conventional education. The nineteenth-century idea that students or apprentices must spend a certain number of hours in a classroom—"butts in seats"—is outdated. New methods of distance education have opened the doors for specialized training that meets the needs of just about everyone.

The overriding advantage is that this specialized and highly-efficient training method puts individuals in the workplace faster and often at a much lower cost. This means that they can start to gain real-world experience sooner and earn incomes that will allow them to accumulate wealth earlier than their predecessors did.[28]

Technology enables educators to incorporate learning techniques that are more time-effective and interactive. The primary purpose is to accelerate learning by allowing students to be involved in the learning process.

Classroom lessons are uniform (one size fits all) and there is no time or resources for a customized and individualized approach. This is a real disadvantage because nobody has the same learning style; for some the instruction may be boring—the pace may not engage the more gifted students. For others it may be too challenging. Technology has created a tool for education to be customized to the needs of every individual.

Technology is streamlining the learning process too. You want to know the money and time you are investing on learning is going to be effective. You want to be sure you can fit the course into your schedule and you can afford it. Today many alternatives exist especially in the area of technical education. Learning a trade in today's economy, as never before in US history, is a practical approach to your career development.

28 "The Entrepreneurial Edge: Companies That Try to Bring Innovative Technology to Teaching," by James Flanigan, *The New York Times,* June 21, 2007.

Technical schools would not exist if colleges delivered the skills needed and were the only resource. Over the last decade, vocational education has become greatly respected. People realize vocational skills training is a practical approach to securing employment, and students can always go back to college at their leisure to study eighteenth-century art with all the wealth and optional time they've created. People are also waking up to the fact that many careers requiring a technical education, but not a college degree, are available.

The potential for success offered by a trade is becoming more widely publicized. In fact, many wealthy people attribute their success to participating in a trade industry.

Yet, unions and other entities have attempted to create barriers to the trade skills training by forcing people to spend unnecessary time and dollars in an apprenticeship program as they wait to become journeymen.

Don't succumb to this artificial requirement. There are effective alternatives to the conventional two- and four-year apprenticeship programs. Don't let people put artificial speed bumps in front of your success.

When compared to a traditional college, there are many benefits to learning from a technical school, including:

- faster learning, with less time commitment
- more specialized programs
- less competition for admissions
- flexible scheduling
- lower cost

Further, there are many certifications and accreditations you may need in the job marketplace that you cannot find at a four-year college. Opportunities for hands-on training and job placement are two other exceptional benefits of many technical trade schools.

Finally, many of the fastest growing professions do not require a college degree. A technical certificate is more than adequate.

A report put out by the National Center for Education Statistics, *Vocational Education in the United States: Toward the Year 2000*, highlights the changes in vocational education in the twenty-first century. Previously vocational education was used to prepare people for entry-level jobs. However, over the last decade there has been a shift toward a higher academic standard for technical education programs.[29]

Vocational education now has a broader purpose and places more emphasis on providing direct-to-market knowledge and experience for a wide range of career choices. This report identifies a clear trend toward more education and training requirements for people entering the workforce.[30]

Certifications from industry associations are often offered at career colleges and technical schools. A certification gives credibility to your skills, and employers are more interested in what you can do for them than where or if you went to school.

Surprisingly, many college graduates still feel the need to obtain certifications after earning their degree to be competitive in the marketplace. If by bypassing the whole college route you can end up with the same job, only four years earlier, then why wouldn't you?

---

29 *Vocational Education in the United States: Toward the Year 2000*. National Center for Education Statistics, February 2000
30 Ibid.

CUT THE COST OF YOUR LEARNING BY AT LEAST HALF JUST BY STAYING HOME

Going away to college is costly, especially when you pay for room and board on top of tuition and books. Having the ability to stay closer to home offers many monetary benefits.

For example, Accelerated Technical Training Institute's home study courses provide the education and facilitate the life balance you need to acquire skills quickly and at a fraction of the cost of conventional education.

One of the most significant benefits of training at a technical institution is the level of dedication to job placement. The goal of a technical school should be to help you get a job. So schools have dedicated career counselors to assist you through the entire job placement process and they may even have industry connections. The best technical schools teach you the skills to do a job and how to find one.

CHAPTER TWELVE

AN EDUCATION THAT CAN PUT YOU ON THE FAST TRACK TO WEALTH

With the popularity and advancement of distance learning, there are more options for learning specific skills than ever before. Online, remote, and speed learning provides the flexibility and financial freedom to gain exactly what you need to be successful without making unnecessarily large investments of time and money.

Distance education is widely recognized by employers as a credible method of teaching and learning. It accelerates the process, getting you started on the right track quickly. A big advantage is that you can fit this type of learning into your schedule and lifestyle. Again, many of the programs cost a small fraction of the cost of attending even one year of college.

So, even if you have decided you are going to college to get a particular degree, a distance education program that teaches you a skill or trade would be a very affordable step. It could provide you the financial vehicle with which to pay for that expensive college degree.

Having skills in an in-demand trade will enable you to command premium wages rather than being stuck at some fast-food joint for minimum wage.

My advice in seeking a career is to pick any trade skill—or ideally, multiple trade skills—that interests you. Learn them quickly and apply your newfound skills to rapidly developing a career. This is your best starting point. Where the road leads you from there is up to your ability to continue to learn while seeking opportunities.

> For trades you can learn quickly through distance education, go to: www.attitradeschools.com

CLASSROOM VERSUS VIDEO AND ONLINE COURSES

In the typical classroom setting, you are extremely lucky if you get twenty minutes of real instruction in an hour-long class. You have probably experienced this. The time is eaten up by the instructor taking roll call and getting ready to teach. Then somebody has to tell a joke or asks a question that takes up time and pulls the class off course. Often the classes are taught to the level of the slowest person in them, thus penalizing and frustrating those who grasp concepts quickly and who are motivated to succeed. To further complicate things, you get a segment of information today which may or may not be complete, and tomorrow, or two days later, or maybe even the next week, the instructor gives you the next segment of information and you have to patch it all together into something that you can comprehend and make use of in the real world.

With distance education and video instruction all the waste is removed and you are able to move at your own pace.

The vast majority of people learn fastest by watching and listening to specific step-by-step instructions.

There are many huge advantages offered by video delivery of distance education. Most people learn best by seeing something done and listening to an explanation. The combination of visual and audio components is very powerful and efficient. If a picture is worth a thousand words, a moving picture is worth many more.

Complex trades can be demonstrated. By watching a video, you can visualize the concept and "get it between your ears." When you see the image of success and what the end result should look like, you can easily teach your hands, with a little practice, the tactile skills needed to achieve the results you desire.

Face it. A "live" instructor can't hold your hands and move them around in order to provide you with the same experience, but, if you can see his or her hands operating close up through video, you can understand the lesson faster than you would when you only listen to a description of the operation or you try reading about it in a book.

Also, Accelerated Technical Training Institute video courses are fully integrated. Information moves seamlessly from point to point in a logical sequence without leaving any gaps in the completion of a specific task. This provides for a better overall learning experience.

Additionally, the ability to play back a particular section for review and retention is another key feature of video instruction that just cannot be replicated in the classroom. With video, students can see features so close up that fingerprints are visible. You certainly wouldn't receive such clear instruction if you sat in a classroom, a few feet away from the instructor—let alone from the back of the classroom—your vision obstructed by other students.

WHY YOU NEED SPEED

I believe that speed is one of the most critical components of success in today's world. You can no longer spend years getting ready to get ready. You need to learn quickly and act. That is why I created the Accelerated Technical Training Institute's unique instructional method. It's a building block technique that enables the average student to learn a skill or trade in a small fraction of the time typically required in a traditional classroom setting.

Learning a trade or skill has never been easier since the introduction of distance learning, which offers programs with a variety of instructional styles designed to deliver education that focuses on a specialized profession.

Teachers and students communicate through electronic media and the subject matter incorporates organization, information management, research, and time management skills.

Distance courses in the trades have been around for more than a hundred years. The first to offer distance learning was Isaac Pitman, who taught shorthand in Great Britain in the 1840s through correspondence. You can also find plumbing courses from the turn of the century.

Throughout the last century, distance learning has changed drastically with the invention of new technology. What is very different today is that rather than having to read a manual or spend years in a trade school, we can now teach much more efficiently through the use of step-by-step video instruction.

Distance learning is not for everyone because it requires a certain level of discipline and self-motivation. However it remains one of the fastest methods to master a subject.

RADICAL ACCELERATED TRAINING

Rapid development is a term used to describe online learning, which employs the shortest possible schedule to learn anything without sacrificing quality. People realize that time is money and there is no point participating in an education program when its learning objectives are not all necessary.

The goal of rapid development learning experiences is to make specialized education better, faster, and cheaper.

Education outside the bricks-and-mortar institution is growing and technology is leading the way with online curricula and a variety of learning software. Advances in distance education have opened up the doors to people who are unable to attend school and offer a way for others to supplement their education. The benefits of online learning vary, but its flexibility remains consistent. There are a lot of choices out there that meet the needs of almost anyone regardless of financial standing, learning capability, and goals. Distance learning courses that target both the trades and business professions are available.

By design and necessity, conventional classroom teaching is not structured to meet the individual needs of every student, and technology is picking up the slack. Online instruction allows you to truly take control of your own education and directly learn the skills you want in order to achieve your specific goals in the workplace.

Different types of distance learning programs are available. They include correspondence through regular mail, Internet delivery, courses broadcast on television or radio, interactive courses using CD ROM, and courses delivered via wireless phones. You have the ability to choose and that is what building your success and wealth is all about. It is not about fitting yourself into a cookie-cutter curriculum;

it is about recognizing your own requirements for education and work success. You do not need to be physically sitting in a classroom to make it happen.

Distance education blends instructional design, project management, and prototyping to expedite the online learning process. This is difficult to do in a classroom setting because you are not required to be in control of the entire process. For instance, in order to be successful with distance education you might need to be able to access your project files from a database or website and create a clear project plan for yourself that incorporates the class schedule and due dates.[31]

Education is no longer looked at in the traditional way. More attention is being paid to the value of a customized approach to accelerate learning. Everybody has his own learning style and personal schedule to accommodate, and now distance education provides alternatives that have the same quality and reputation as a traditional college campus. You cannot underestimate the value of real-life work experience when looking for employment, and distance education provides you the opportunity to combine education and employment simultaneously.

There is no point in taking courses or programs that only incorporate a portion of the skills you are trying to learn. There are many college degree programs that require you to take prerequisites that do not have anything to do with the career path you have chosen. Online learning and vocational institutions provide a more focused and specialized approach to education that allows you to fast-track your career.

Today, online degrees are considered valid by prospective employers whose attitude about distance learning has changed.

31 "Online Learning for Tough Times: Keys to Rapid Development" by Ed Mayberry, Learning Circuits online, astd.org.

Many of the best schools in the country offer online degree courses. Employers look for demonstrated skills and experience that will make you a great candidate. You can even take an MBA course online, which is a great indication of the strength of the reputation of distance learning.

Even when a college offers distance learning, there is no point in spending thousands of dollars attending the college course if you can achieve the same thing at your own pace and at a price that does not put you into years of debt. A highly targeted education combined with work experience is the most effective way to fast track your success.

The money you save by educating yourself through online learning allows you to get involved in other things that are valuable to your life and career. Not only can you gain work experience, but also you have the time and money to have a life. You can travel or get involved in your community, which are both great resume boosters, and best of all you will have more time for yourself. Working and attending a college campus simultaneously is possible, but doing so in your own time is more realistic and a lot less stressful. You do not have to sacrifice other things you want to do, which will make you happier in the long run. Less stress means paying more attention to learning.

Eric Hebert assists students with research techniques and web publishing skills to help them track and document their education online. Hebert says, "It's time for students and businesses to evolve with technology. In this online global economy, it's conceivable for a mom and pop business to run circles around a large corporation because of the flexibility and reach of the Internet. It's also feasible for a student to more effectively demonstrate their abilities and knowledge using the web. It really is a level playing field, and if you don't embrace and utilize these techniques, your competition surely will."[32]

Hebert also highlights an important fact that today's working world is full of "forward thinking business" employers and they are seeking "like-minded people." Higher education programs from online education provide people with the experience, the technology, and the skills to be independent contributors. In today's workplace employers want people who can bring ideas to the table and think outside the box. Online learning forces students to think for themselves and acquire self-discipline and perseverance. Hebert describes online education students as "totally in control of their academic destiny." This highlights the additional, valuable skill sets gained through online education. Online students control when they study and when they graduate. Employers look for individuals, not groups of people with the same college degree certificate. The key is dedication. When you are in charge of your own education, it is easier to invest in it and communicate your accomplishments when it counts.[33]

There has been criticism that online learning lacks the same warmth as the traditional classroom, but changes are being made to make it more interpersonal. Today there is a higher level of instructor interaction by e-mail and video conferencing as well as online chat rooms for students to communicate with each other. This has increased interaction, taking away the stigma of isolation. There are also other forms of assistance that online schools provide for students, whether for solving technical problems or for addressing

32 Eric Hebert, http://evolvor.com.
33 "15 Reasons Why You Don't Need to Attend an 'Elite' College," May 7, 2007, http://www.collegedegree.com/library/college-choice/elite-college.

general concerns. Essentially, you are not on your own to the extent that you have to solve all of your problems yourself.

The level of satisfaction gained from taking online courses can vary, but probably the most obvious is that those who learn online have much more freedom to accommodate their studies to their own personal schedules. Many students taking distance learning classes also have full- or part-time jobs, and are sometimes parents too. The freedom that comes with taking classes online is something that is definitely unmatched by classroom courses. This alone in recent years has been a big motivation for people seeking an education while living a busy life.

A report was published following a 1999–2000 survey conducted by the National Center for Education Statistics in which students who participated in distance education were asked, "Compared to other courses you've taken, are you more satisfied, equally satisfied, or less satisfied with the quality of instruction you've received in your distance education courses?" The results showed that approximately half were "equally satisfied" with their distance education and their regular classroom. The survey found that a little more than 20 percent of the students were "more satisfied" and approximately 30 percent were "less satisfied." According to Hebert, the survey showed that "the quality of online education has remained consistent, while allowing people to feel they have accomplished their educational goals."[34]

34 "The Satisfaction of Taking Online Courses," http://www.collegeonline.org/library/distance-vs-local/online-course-satisfaction.html.

CHAPTER THIRTEEN

A CASE STUDY IN POOR CHOICES

Creating success and wealth is not just about asking yourself what you want to "be." You might want to start by asking yourself what you don't want to be.

You need to be clear about what you won't do for money. You also need to peer into your future and try to determine if you would be happy continuing to do a specific job in twenty years.

As you go through this process of "being and not being," minimize your costs, hold off on the college decision, find other avenues to explore your career choice, and engage in training to help you make your decision.

This is important because college can be an escape for many students who do not know what they want to do, believe in the college myth, and succumb to college marketing pitches. It is an expensive place to hide from the real world and the real world will not be any less intimidating when you get out. In fact, it can provide a worse scenario as you enter a difficult job market where you need to work to pay off your debt rather than start saving and investing.

Remember, If you don't know exactly how college will get you a job, then how do you know that it will at all?

AN INDIVIDUAL CASE STUDY: "POVERTY, THE RESULT OF MISGUIDED COLLEGE EDUCATION," A TRUE STORY BY HERBERT W. PAHLOW

It was a weekday evening at our three-bedroom ranch home in Roland, Iowa. The doorbell rang. A tall, thin stranger stood at the door. He had answered our ad in the newspaper for "Home for Sale by Owner," and had called us to make an appointment to visit my wife and me.

By the time he left, we had agreed to sell our house to him. After closing the deal, I drove the fifty miles to the mortgage company in Waterloo, Iowa. I arrived at 4:45 p.m. on a Friday and paid off the mortgage just fifteen minutes before it would go into total default.

It was the fall of 1977 and I had been fired from Sundstrand Hydro-Transmission in Ames, Iowa. I was unemployed with a wife and three small kids to support. Our money was running out fast, so we sold the house.

In 1983, 1995, and 2006, we lost three more homes because we could not get them sold before they went into foreclosure. Each home loss was preceded by a lengthy period of unemployment.

When we lost the four homes, we lost all the down-payment money, loan origination costs, and equity. The 1995 loss came when we were just five years from paying it off.

Why have I experienced so much unemployment and financial loss after being an honor student in high school and graduating from college?

Years of contemplation on this question and an analysis of the events has brought me to the conclusion that college is not for everyone and can actually do more harm than good if it is not the right fit for you.

Along the way I found statistics that claimed college graduates earn on average a million more dollars in a lifetime than people without a degree. But what if you are one of those who pull down the average with long bouts of unemployment?

My "extra million dollars" was erased by the losses caused by unemployment. You need to look at the long-term effects of a career decision. It doesn't pay to earn money if you cannot keep any of it. One step forward and two steps backward is not progress.

Career decisions should not be made haphazardly but with explicit planning after careful analysis. Part of that analysis should include a consideration of what other people say about your abilities. It should also include a professional career evaluation. It amazes me that I did not take a career evaluation test until forty-two years after high school.

How did college hurt me financially? The answer to this question is multifaceted, but it started with the wrong college choice.

Late in life I came to realize that it did not matter which college I had attended. I based this thinking upon the lives of many people I observed in the workplace.

I chose Case Tech, which later became Case Western Reserve University. The prestige of attending Case Institute of Technology had captured my mind. I graduated in 1968 with a BS degree in physics. I don't remember meeting anyone there who was not first in his or her class in high school.

The tuition was very high compared with other possible choices. If I had chosen the University of Cincinnati, and gone through the "co-op" program, the tuition debt at graduation would have been far smaller.

There were two factors affecting this: lower tuition rates, and employment 50 percent of each year rather than 25 percent. In that co-op program you had school for three months and a job for three months, rather than nine months of school and three months of work. But attendance at any college entails such high costs that it had better be worth it.

It took me sixteen years to pay off five-sixths of my tuition debt. When I needed a job, I noticed that most job applications asked for my college grade point average, which was barely above C. The debt consumed too much of my pay, and the low-grade point average made it more difficult for me to get a job. The problem of low college grades has haunted me for almost forty years.

Nowadays I hear of people graduating with more than $50,000 of debt. I also have observed that college grants and scholarships are usually only offered along with substantial student loans. This means that you cannot avoid debt entirely, and if you do, your parents probably used their home equity as collateral for your education. If that is the case, you may be responsible for supporting them when they are old and broke.

During some of my periods of unemployment when I couldn't obtain a college-level job, I tried to find a lower-level job to help pay the bills. Most of the time, these employers ignored me. Sometimes I was told that I was "overqualified." This meant that the employer thought I would stay on the job only until something better came along, so the employer hired someone else. When my college degree couldn't get me a good job, it kept me from getting any kind of job.

Another problem that I faced was the changing supply and demand for the college-level jobs I was seeking. I thought that I had found a niche when I had several stretches of employment in quality and reliability engineering, which lasted a total of about ten years. But the federal government implemented huge defense expenditure reductions in the late 1980s that put a glut of quality engineers into the job market. I was laid off along with 2,500 employees from Northrop-Grumman in 1988.

I thought that I had found another niche when my eighteen-year career in information technology ended, following the crash of dot com stocks in the early 2000s. That put the oversupply of computer specialists on the unemployment rolls.

When I applied in 2004 for a job as an information technology manager at a boys ranch in New London, Wisconsin, there was no response (as usual) after waiting a couple of months. So I called to inquire about my application. The director of human resources told me they had received sixty applications for the position. "Would you like to be a house parent?" he asked. My wife and I took the job as house parents, but it only lasted fourteen months. It was a job mismatch.

Unemployment is a compounding problem. When you can't get a job, you can't pay your bills. When you can't pay your bills, your credit rating gets damaged, and the negative history stays on your record for seven years.

When you apply for jobs requiring a college degree, employers can check your credit (with or without your permission). If you have a bad credit history, they ignore you. You are stuck, broke, and desperate. Because of the credit checks, you can't rent an apartment or borrow money to buy a car to get to work.

No job means more unpaid bills and an even worse credit rating. So don't start down that road in the first place. Start with a career evaluation test. You need a career choice that will get you on top of the competition in your chosen field.

Reread the previous sentence.

During layoffs, employers keep the best and fire the rest.

All of the jobs I have mentioned thus far required a college degree. I think any post-high school training needs to be matched to your natural talents, interests, and career goals. If you want to be a doctor, dentist, or lawyer in the USA, of course you must go to college. If you want to be a military career officer, of course you must go to college.

When I analyzed the lives of my brothers, sisters, wife, children, and friends, I realized that they had stable careers with increasingly better pay and no unemployment. No, they did not take career evaluation tests, but I think it doesn't hurt to confirm the direction in which you are going. The undesirable consequences of career mismatch are not worth the risks. Everyone doesn't naturally fall into his or her ideal career field.

My wife, Polly, went through a one-year training program (with no tuition debt) to be a licensed practical nurse. Her career choice fit for her talents and personality very well. In forty years, she has never had trouble getting or keeping a job at high pay. Today she works for Medicaid as a private duty nurse contractor.

Our son, Jason, only went through eighth grade, but he acquired on-the-job training in ceramic tile installation at age fifteen. For the past twenty years, he has always had work and has never been unemployed. Now he has his own successful business.

He is so skilled in his work that he is sometimes asked to do ceramic or marble tile for massive homes with indoor underground swimming pools and underground tennis courts in Green Bay, Wisconsin. Since he bought his own house a few years ago, he has made many cash improvements to it. He also owns four acres of land in two parcels in the Wisconsin North Woods. He has two pick-up trucks, an ATV, and a nice Honda motorcycle. He only owes money on the real estate, on which he is making accelerated payments.

Our daughter, Rhoda, has a natural talent for identifying vintage clothing. She buys vintage clothing in the Nashville area and re-sells it on E-bay. Because of her uncanny ability, she can buy very low and sell very high.

As a father, I had fits when she was dating David, who was working as an orderly in a nursing home. Then she married him. David became an apprentice electrician to learn the trade for residential electrical work. One of his employers paid for him to attend night classes for four years to become a master electrician. Now, at age thirty-seven, he is a superintendent of foremen who oversee commercial electrical projects in the Nashville area. He has never experienced unemployment, gets paid well, and has no education debt.

When my brother, Mark, was living at home with my parents during high school, he read the entire World Book Encyclopedia at home to educate himself about life. During summers and after high school graduation he traveled to Europe, supporting himself with jobs in various countries. He has continued his life education by being an avid reader, even now, but he has never gone to college.

Years ago he started a business in Seattle, selling things to make people laugh. Sales traditionally were from a retail store and a mail-order catalog. He traveled to China and other foreign countries to contract with manufacturers to make his uniquely original products. Now his business is international with more than fifty employees.

LEARNING FROM HERBERT'S STORY

Hebert's experience makes the case very well, and his experience is not unlike so many others out there struggling right now, wondering what happened to their successful life and wealth.

In sharing his struggle, Herbert can help countless people make smart career decisions. This true story is a perfect example of why it is important to do your research and explore all of your options, before making a "guaranteed" success of your life by attending college.

MY ADVICE TO CAREER SEEKERS

A s you can see, attending college does not guarantee success and wealth and can be an expensive myth for you and the herd to believe in.

The facts discussed in this book and available elsewhere "out there" tells us that college isn't the only or best option for many people. They show us that things have changed in this country, and now more than ever there is a huge possibility that attending college for the wrong reasons, or for careers where there just isn't opportunity—unbeknownst to the unwary—will lead to massive debt and frustration, not wealth and creation.

My mission is to give you hope and a solution by encouraging you to look carefully at the most important decisions of your life, your career, and wealth creation, so you can not only survive but also thrive. And, as you explore your options, consider learning in-demand trade skills to avoid becoming just another college graduate out of work and in debt.

Especially consider learning multiple trades for foundational money-making skills, so you are prepared to take advantage of any opportunity in the marketplace in good economic times and bad.

Trade work is needed in this country as never before, and we aren't training our workforce to take advantage of this vast opportunity. Trade work can't be shipped overseas, and as a skilled trade technician you'll always have something you can do to make money that survives the test of time and gives you the most flexibility, putting you in control of your career, your wealth, and your life.

Steps to get your career and wealth creation on the right track:

1. Start with a career evaluation and take the test available on my website at www.instantjobskills.com.

2. Get opinions on your natural talents from teachers, guidance counselors, parents, grandparents, and others. Write them down and review them.

3. Shape your career objectives and develop a plan of action that minimizes debt. Write them down and review them.

4. Research and obtain the most affordable, high-quality training you need to accomplish your objectives. You'll always need training of some kind, so make life-long learning your goal.

5. Live at home with parents while training if possible, or work while training, if you can successfully balance both.

6. Get placed in an appropriate job, in line with your objectives and training.

7. Automatically save 10 percent of your income for the rest of your life without spending any of it ever. When the amount gets really large, you will need professional

advice to keep from losing it and to keep it growing. Hire a financial advisor with a reputable firm so your money is secure.

8. Eventually the pile of money you create with compound interest will grow faster than the rate of inflation. Set up special savings funds for things you want later, such as cars or houses.

9. In life you will either work for money, or money will work for you. You will have both experiences while you are saving. Investing money works for you like duplicating yourself in the workplace.

10. If, after you have some years of experience and you become an expert in your field, consider self-employment. It is possible that you can make more money from your own business than from working for an employer

11. Slow and steady wins the race. The turtle always wins against the rabbit.

There you have it.

Don't go to college unless:

1. it is the only way that you can utilize your natural talents;

2. you can only achieve specific goals through attendance;

3. you can do it with minimal debt.

Consider the fact that you can go far in life without college if you train for the right career, and are wise with your money. Start sooner rather than later.

For more information on training in multiple trades through my company, Accelerated Technical Training Institute at www.attitradeschools.com, see "Taking the First Step: Speed Learning the Seven Trades Through the Accelerated Technical Training Institute" at the back of this book.

TAKING THE
FIRST STEP

SPEED LEARNING THE SEVEN TRADES
THROUGH THE ACCELERATED
TECHNICAL TRAINING INSTITUTE

WHY LEARN THE TRADES?

According to the National Inflation Association's report, *How a Bubble has Developed in the Cost of Education*, college costs have gone up because the government interfered with the free market by providing long-term educational loans that are easy to qualify for.

Just like the housing bubble of 2004-2008, this has encouraged excessive borrowing with a potentially poor return on investment and a lot of personal debt.

The vast amount of easily obtained funding available to prospective house buyers who shouldn't have been considered for loans, and the large number of buyers in the market place, drove prices higher and higher until the market bust. It was a house of cards, so it collapsed. Today, college funding is no different. It is just another bubble on the verge of exploding, and many of those who have invested too much in it, will lose their investment. Meanwhile, the USA is crumbling around our ears as bridges, roads, pipelines, electrical grids, and more decay and fail. Who is going to rebuild our country?

The need for skilled individuals who can rebuild our infrastructure has never been higher, yet not enough workers are being trained. In fact, most skilled tradesmen are in their late 60s and 70s and, sadly, passing away. They are physically unable to work anymore.

We now have a situation in which the need for skilled labor is steadily growing, yet the current generation has practically no trade skills. Workers have not been taught a real trade, let alone a series of trades that would always provide them with the ability to create employment and income.

People who possess multiple trade skills are in demand and their wages are rising. Small and big companies, governments, and Americans from all walks of life need people with these trade skills to provide them with critical infrastructure repairs.

WHY ACCELERATED TECHNICAL TRAINING INSTITUTE?

The institute's **Certified Multitrade Technician (CMTT)**™ Program is about building your competence in **the seven trades** so you have the confidence to address any situation and do the work. You will be competent enough to say, "I can fix that … I can do that job," while enjoying the respect of your peers, possessing in-demand job skills, and having a foundation you can build on for the rest of your life to create success and wealth your own way.

> "They laughed when I said I could repair anything.
> But then they stood aside and watched in awe as
> I got out my tools and went to work."

THE CMTT™ PROGRAM INCLUDES TRAINING
IN ALL OF THE SEVEN TRADES:

- Electrical contracting

- Plumbing

- Carpentry

- Masonry

- Welding

- Machining

- Locksmithing

AS A CERTIFIED MULTITRADE TECHNICIAN
(CMTT)™ STUDENT YOU WILL

- Quickly develop competency in the seven trades;

- Get CMTT certification in a fraction of the time and cost of traditional educational institutions;

- Command respect with a vast array of proven skills in multiple trades;

- Be certified for a high-paying career track;

- Quickly become an authority in your field;

- Engage in an accelerated learning experience;

- Receive consistent, high-level instruction from trade experts;

- Not have to leave home or quit your current job during training;

- Learn at a pace you control;

- Avoid the down time associated with classroom learning;

- Learn primarily by video and hands-on training with minimal reading required;

- Always have close-up views of the instruction;

- Find the cost very affordable, especially when compared to many colleges;

- Control your destiny; take the learning process into your own hands with a method to accelerate it;

- Experience an exclusive and unique offering; no one can compare with the Accelerated Technical Training Institute, and as a result of your membership, no one will compare with you;

- Overcome the college myth and build your future by becoming a Certified Multitrade Technician through the Accelerated Technical Training Institute and start rebuilding America.

The Accelerated Technical Training Institute's instructors are world-class experts. They are the best in the business, averaging twenty-five to thirty-five years of experience. They are carefully selected for their ability to explain advanced technology in a readily understandable manner.

Call one of our helpful Accelerated Technical Training Institute enrollment counselors or visit our website today.

www.attitradeSchools.com

707.253.1447

How can you use this book?

MOTIVATE

EDUCATE

THANK

INSPIRE

PROMOTE

CONNECT

Why have a custom version of *The College Myth*?

- Build personal bonds with customers, prospects, employees, donors, and key constituencies
- Develop a long-lasting reminder of your event, milestone, or celebration
- Provide a keepsake that inspires change in behavior and change in lives
- Deliver the ultimate "thank you" gift that remains on coffee tables and bookshelves
- Generate the "wow" factor

Books are thoughtful gifts that provide a genuine sentiment that other promotional items cannot express. They promote employee discussions and interaction, reinforce an event's meaning or location, and they make a lasting impression. Use your book to say "Thank You" and show people that you care.

The College Myth is available in bulk quantities and in customized versions at special discounts for corporate, institutional, and educational purposes. To learn more please contact our Special Sales team at:

1.866.775.1696 • sales@advantageww.com • www.AdvantageSpecialSales.com

Printed in the USA
CPSIA information can be obtained
at www.ICGtesting.com
JSHW051958150824
68134JS00056B/3187

9 781599 321004